For Marie,
who suffered
with me through the
Jeanie Johnston's
prolonged birth pangs
and never lost faith--
in Jeanie, or in me

ACKNOWLEDGMENTS

The number of people to whom I owe a debt of gratitude is astounding: Tony Esposito, Carl Olbrich, Hank Malek and George Woodford, original crew members of *Second Wind*, who helped restore my spirit; Gus Bruns, whose curiosity about all things Irish sparked my interest in the *Jeanie Johnston;* Helen Ryle, my faithful email pen pal who was my eyes and ears in Ireland, and from whom I quote extensively; John Griffin, the visionary whose optimism sprang eternal; Turlough McConnell, Michael O'Carroll and Mike Forwood, who, each in his own way, articulated the vision; Tom McCarthy, Rob Matthews, Rowan MacSweeney, Tom Harding, Peter O'Regan and others who helped me live out the fantasy; many fellow United States Coast Guard Auxiliarists, especially Bob Myers, Fred Gates and Mel Borofsky, who opened doors for me, and members of my Flotilla 16-10, 5NR, whose encouragement and support never faltered; Jackie Hill, Carolan Ammirata and other dedicated health professionals at the Life Fitness Center who helped me hold the ravages of age at bay; Millie Munroe, who read my manuscript and offered helpful advice; Rutgers University Class of '42 classmates who urged me on; and dozens of other friends among Rutgers alumni, faculty and staff; the Riverview Seniors of Brielle and the Manasquan River Yacht Club who may have thought I was crazy but never said so.

PHOTO CREDITS Cover: Paul Dolan; Back cover, top: Tom Harding; All shipyard photos (following p. 52): Helen Ryle; Voyage photos (following p. 146): 1st page, top: Tom Harding; 2nd page, bottom: Tash Treacy.

Wilt Thou steer my frail black bark
O'er the dark broad ocean's foam?
Wilt Thou come, Lord, to my boat,
Where afloat, my will would roam?
Thine the mighty; Thine the small:
Thine to mark men fall, like rain;
God! wilt Thou grant aid to me
Who came o'er th' upheaving main?

Irish, 9th Century
Cormac, King-Bishop of Cashel, *The Heavenly Pilot*
Translated by George Sigerson

The pain suffered in the Jeanie Johnston project
will make the Jeanie a very desirable visitor to
American ports. They will be quite interested in
visiting a ship that rose from the dead three times
before her sails were unfurled.

Irish, 21st Century
Padraig Kennelly, writing in *Kerry's Eye*

CONTENTS

CHAPTER 1
The Dream Takes Shape

WHEN I first saw the *Jeanie Johnston*, she was not much to look at. What there was of her was sitting in a small remote shipyard hidden behind a row of storefronts in a village on the west coast of Ireland.

My first thought was that the clusters of wooden beams I saw there were either a wood sculpture or a set of giant tuning forks advertising, perhaps, a music festival. It would have taken a leap of faith to know that these were the first frames of a wooden ship, that they would be joined by many more frames, all bolted to a keel, and that the whole assembly would eventually be enclosed in planking to define a ship's hull.

Whatever they were, there was something naked and forlorn about them as they rose up from the surrounding clutter, struggling to become something I didn't know about, something I didn't yet understand.

Almost stranger than the appearance of the embryonic ship was the way I was introduced to it. It's too simplistic to say it was serendipity. Say rather that I was guided. It's happened before. There's a little nudge from somewhere offstage-- call it a hunch-- that tells you there's a new door opening, a new avenue to explore, a right way to go. You can fail to recognize it and miss the opportunity, or you can follow it and change your life.

I have puzzled for years over why, as I approached the edge of a ruined stone wall of a farmhouse in an Italian field almost 60 years ago, I walked to the left rather than to the right. Like Robert Frost's road less traveled, the path I took made all the difference.

Looming on a hilltop ahead was the Abbey of Montecassino reputed to be a German artillery observation post. As I walked abreast of the wall, an 88 mm artillery shell burst on the opposite side, no more than three feet away. Had I walked to the right, I would not be telling this story today.

There are those who believe that all is luck, and in such a random universe as ours I come close to their side but am not entirely on it. At the other extreme are those who are certain their every footstep is guided. I cannot accept that God favors me over any other being, so their viewpoint can not be mine. But between the two, there must surely be occasional moments, at the intersection of time and eternity, when a slight influence, angelic or otherwise, may shift our footsteps in one direction or another.

It was such a little nudge, I'm sure, that brought me to the *Jeanie Johnston*. My wife Marie and I were on a walking tour of Ireland. Our tour bus was taking us to the Dingle Peninsula, where we would climb mountains, explore Iron Age forts, view early Christian monastic sites and feast our eyes on some of the most spectacular seascapes anywhere. But first we stopped at Blennerville, near the foot of the peninsula, for lunch.

"We leave at one o'clock," said our tour guide. The restaurant was crowded, and it took time to be served. When we'd finished, we had about 10 minutes before bus time, and Marie elected to browse in the gift shop.

I picked up a handful of tourist folders and was about to join her when something prompted me to head outdoors.

The principal attraction of Blennerville is its historic windmill, built in 1800. There was a windmill museum and tours of the windmill itself, but I had no time for either. With only minutes left, I started walking toward the bus but was suddenly attracted to a dwindling dirt road at the edge of the village that was obviously going nowhere, and for some reason that even then I couldn't explain, began to follow it. I came to a tall fence, and through an opening I saw those strange-looking clusters of wooden beams. I wandered into the enclosure.

"You can't come in here," said a man who was obviously a guard. "You'll have to go to the Visitor Center around front."

I didn't have time for that. "What's happening here?" I asked. "It's the *Jeanie Johnston* Project," said the guard. "They're building a tall ship here. She'll be the pride of Ireland when she's finished." The wooden beams were the ribs of the ship, and they looked like nothing but a jumble of timbers.

"Thank you," I said, looking at my watch and edging away. If I had known then how profoundly those odd-looking assemblages of wood were eventually to impact my life, I might have studied them more carefully. But my time was up.

On my way to the parking lot, I glanced across the street and saw a sign, "*Jeanie Johnston* Visitor Center." Unfortunately, I wouldn't get to see it.

As the bus pulled out, I looked at the folders I'd collected. One of them described the *Jeanie Johnston* Project. The *Jeanie Johnston*, I learned, had sailed the North American route in the 19th Century, when millions of people fled famine-ravaged Ireland, most of them headed for new lives in the US and Canada. She was a "tall ship," a three-masted barque in the last days of pure sail before steam power took over the sea lanes.

Now the Irish were resurrecting the *Jeanie Johnston*. A full-size replica, perfect in every detail, would be constructed there in the shipyard at Blennerville by shipwrights from many countries. The call had gone out for those who could still work wood the old-fashioned way, and young apprentices were being gathered from Ireland and Northern Ireland to work side-by-side with them to learn the old skills before they died out.

The wooden beams I had glimpsed were massive timbers of

3

Irish oak, hewn and shaped by hand to form the frames that would make up the skeleton of the ship. When they were all cut, assembled and fastened to the ship's keel, the work of planking and decking would begin. It would be wood all the way, with hand tools, the way it was done in the 1840s, when the original *Jeanie Johnston* was built. There would not be a square inch of fiberglass in the hull of this ship.

Why was it all being done? The year 2000 was roughly the 150th anniversary of the great exodus from Ireland-- the "famine years" brought on by the failure of the Irish potato crop, and the *Jeanie Johnston* Project would commemorate that defining moment in Irish history. It would also call attention to Ireland's maritime heritage, and in the words of the folder I was reading, "link Ireland, North and South, Unionist and Nationalist traditions; link Ireland with her extended communities in the United States and Canada and harness the good will for Ireland that exists in Britain, Continental Europe and North America."

The next question was: Would they be able to do it, or was it a quixotic dream? I had read about some of the problems encountered by builders of replica ships elsewhere. What I saw here were many brave words, but how would they assemble the raw materials, and how would they find the shipwrights skilled at wooden ship building?

Ireland, as the Millennial Year approached, was feeling her oats, and well she might. On our tour of the western counties, traditionally the nation's most remote and impoverished, we saw not an empty storefront anywhere. Business was booming, Ireland's years of membership in the European Union (while Britain still debated and dawdled) was paying off in grants and trade, and the old curse of emigration was beginning to reverse.

For the first time anyone could recall, talented young people-- artists, musicians, actors, managers-- who had fled their native land for a better life in the New World-- were starting to return home. A burgeoning economy was producing money to provide the employment opportunities and support the arts in a way

4

that had never happened before.

The *Jeanie Johnston* would be a symbol of all this.

In a way, the Irish were coming to terms with their history, looking at it dispassionately and examining it in ways they had never really done before. Looking back at the bad old days was easier, of course, when you could do it from the perspective of good times.

You could see the new attitude in the gift shops. Leprechauns were becoming hard to find. Instead of souvenir trinkets of the little people, the shops were featuring original Irish arts and crafts. But the leprechauns had only gone underground, as I was to learn-- to my dismay-- in the months ahead.

I had read some Irish history and knew in a general way the story of the famine years and the great emigration. My own grandmother had been a 19th Century émigré from Ireland. Jo-anna O'Brien was born in County Cork in 1847 and emigrated to the US-- alone, penniless and illiterate-- at age 16.

My father never talked much about his parents, and by the time I had reached the point where genealogy interested me, he was long gone and beyond reach of my questions. Where in Cork was she born? Why did she emigrate at such a youthful age? What about the rest of her family?

She died before I was born, so I never saw her. All I have are some fading snapshots taken on Memorial Day, 1914, when she would have been 67. She is dressed in a long black gown that buttoned tight around her neck, her hair is drawn back in a knot, and on her head is a squat, cylinder-shaped black hat. But it's the face that draws attention. It's a strong face, with heavy brows, wide-set eyes and a square jaw.

One might be inclined to sympathize with the fragility of a 16-year-old girl traveling alone to a strange new world, but when I look at those direct eyes and that square jaw, I know this was a woman who, even at 16, knew how to take care of herself. What the photos show is a feisty old lady who has seen a lot and weathered it all. She never did learn to read or write, but she raised a family whose members succeeded in America in ways their forebears never could in Ireland, and she must have been proud of that.

The only other thing I know about her is the most charming of all. When my mother and father were married, she took off her shoes and stockings and danced barefoot at their wedding reception, shocking my mother's proper German relatives.

Our Irish walking tour had started in Limerick, and we'd arranged to arrive there several days early. I'd hoped we might have time to do a little research on Joanna O'Brien-- perhaps learn what town she was born in, and maybe unearth some old family records.

On one of our free days, we drove south into Cork. I had called the Cork County Heritage Center and found the staff there amazingly obliging. The woman I talked to offered to do a computer search while I was on the phone. Over the next five minutes, she came up with four or five Joanna O'Briens, but none born in 1847. "Our records aren't all on computer yet," she said, "but you might try the Mallow Heritage Center."

We passed through Mallow on our way south and saw the Heritage Center, but unfortunately it was closed for the weekend. Our destination was Cobh, the port town near Cork City. It was almost certainly the port where my grandmother would have embarked, and I had long wanted to see Cobh's famous emigration museum, The Queenstown Story.

Cobh has had more than its share of tragic maritime history. In 1912 it was the last stop for the *Titanic* before the ship left for its rendezvous with a giant iceberg. The *Lusitania* was torpedoed and sunk by a German submarine off the coast nearby in 1915. And for more than a century, Cobh was the main port from which Irish emigrants left for America. Almost six million left between 1848 and 1950, two and a half million of them from Cobh. No wonder it was called the "Gateway of Tears."

The museum's exhibits and audiovisual displays painted a heart-wrenching picture. Standing in front of them, you can easily imagine you are one of the poverty-stricken horde crammed into ships so crowded and unsanitary that thousands died en route, never getting to see the New World. The name these vessels were given-- "coffin ships"-- tells the whole story.

I pictured Joanna O'Brien, a country girl of 16, standing on the quay at Cobh, saying tearful farewells to her family, whom, no doubt, she would never see again. Being illiterate herself, there would be no letters home unless she could get someone to write them for her. She must have been full of uncertainty, and some fear, about what lay ahead.

By the time we were ready to drive back to Limerick, it was dark. Driving on the wrong side of the road with an unfamiliar stick shift was bad enough; I had never done it at night. The width of Irish country roads probably has not changed since the days of horse carts, and with encroaching brush and overhanging trees, they seem narrower than they are. Oncoming trucks seemed bent on sweeping me off the road, and I cringed each time one approached.

How in the world, I thought, are the Irish going to cope with their increased car ownership and traffic that prosperity was sure to bring them? The little roads can hardly bear the traffic they have now, and there's sure to be lots more coming.

Somehow I managed to get us back safely to our hotel. The next day-- the first day of our tour-- was the day the bus took us to Blennerville, and fate-- if that's what it was-- led me to the shipyard where the *Jeanie Johnston* was being built.

The days that followed were a visual and emotional feast of Ireland. We toured ancient estates, walked the spectacular cliffs of Moher and followed the manicured trails of Kylemore Abbey. We explored the strange limestone wilderness of The Burren, climbed a mountain to St. Patrick's Spring and hiked around two islands-- Inishmore in the Aran Islands and Omey Island, inhabited so long that the waves keep washing human bones out of the sand. But there was no opportunity to learn more about my grandmother or the *Jeanie Johnston*.

7

A few weeks after we returned from Ireland, I was searching for a story to fill the newsletter I edited for the Coast Guard Auxiliary when I came across the *Jeanie Johnston* folder. My readers were all interested in boats and the sea, so I ran a brief article and an accompanying photo of the shipyard.

Some months later-- early in 1999-- I happened on a friend who had read about the shipbuilding project, and he said he'd heard they were starting to assemble a crew.

Mostly out of curiosity, I wrote to the shipyard, enclosing a copy of the Coast Guard Auxiliary newsletter. I told them how I'd come upon the ship during our tour and said I'd like to know what their crew requirements were. I had no idea what I expected, or what I might do.

After about three weeks, a letter arrived from Ireland. "Regarding your enquiry for crew positions on the *Jeanie Johnston*," it said, "the crew will be chosen by the master of the ship. To date a master has not been appointed but we have a considerable number of applicants and plan to interview them later on in May."

It went on to say that the ship would be licensed to carry 40 people-- 28 crew and 12 fee-paying passengers. "The crew will be chosen by the master but will include some young people from Ireland North and South who will undergo sail training throughout the coming year. If you are interested in a crew position, we suggest you forward us a copy of your CV outlining your sailing qualifications, etc., which will be forwarded to the ·master in due course."

Also enclosed was a handsome kit with a booklet and background information on the construction of the ship and the planned voyage.

The original *Jeanie Johnston* was a cut above the coffin ships of her day. At a time when overcrowding and disease were standard on emigrant ships, she was a well-run, well-maintained ship that never lost a passenger to disease or to the sea.

During the famine years, the still-young American nation had stiffer maritime requirements than the aging British empire. The US allowed only two passengers per five tons of the vessel's registered tonnage. By contrast, British coffin ships allowed three passengers for every five tons. The overcrowding that resulted was a prime factor in the spread of disease. *Jeanie I* hewed to the American regulations and so was legally permitted into US ports.

Naturally, the fares on the coffin ships were cheaper, and, as always, the poor suffered the most. Fares from Ireland to America ranged from $12 to $60 or so, the latter if you could afford a cabin. If an emigrant had little cash, or his landlord wanted troublesome tenants off the land by the cheapest means, he'd be more likely to end up in Canada than the US.

Even so, once they got there-- if they survived-- famine emigrants by the thousands headed south and walked across the border into the US, where the railroads and canals were being built and there were jobs for poor Irishmen.

When *Jeanie II* arrived in the US-- if the Project succeeded-- she would be carrying all that history with her, in addition to a wealth of genealogical data, so the descendants of the canal diggers and railroad builders would be able to trace their ancestors' roots and follow their voyages.

Irish/Americans by the thousands were expected to flock to the docks, and the Ancient Order of Hibernians and other Irish interest groups would be mounting parades, exhibitions and folk celebrations.

The Project was a visionary one, and I found it historically interesting if not fascinating, but the letter about my potential part in it raised more questions than it answered. The distinction between passengers and crew wasn't clear, for one thing. And with no captain yet in sight, it would be months before any applications would even be seen by an authoritative person. The whole project began to sound like pie in the sky.

Time went by. We enjoyed a February bareboat charter in the British Virgin Islands with daughter Nancy and son-in-law

Brooks, then a summer of sailing on our own boat, *Second Wind*, in the Chesapeake.

It was fall of 1999 now-- a year after my encounter with those strange wooden ribs in the Irish shipyard-- and as the end of the year, decade, century and millennium approached, I still had sailing on my mind. What could I do to celebrate this milestone in a unique way that somehow involved being under sail?

The coming of the millennium had engaged the attention of millions of people, in thousands of different ways. Going up on a mountaintop and waiting for all the computers to crash didn't sound like much fun; neither did standing in front of the Great Pyramid in a captive audience of three million, watching a sound and light show.

I thought of Foxy's, the ultimate yachtsman's hangout in the British Virgins. We'd stopped there on a quiet day for a drink, and as we surveyed the hundreds of t-shirts hanging from the rafters that gave Foxy's its distinctive ambience, we had been told that as many as a hundred boats typically made the place their New Year's Eve raft-up destination.

I called Rick at the company we'd chartered with and quickly sensed negative vibrations. "You should have thought of it months ago," he said. "Everyone else did, and there's not a boat available." What's more, he added, this New Year's Eve was going to be the wildest ever. Some 300 boats were expected to converge on the beach bar, and late-comers would have to walk boat-to-boat for half a mile to get ashore. In a normal year, Rick said, a half dozen people were injured, some with broken limbs, as they fell between boats.

So much for that idea. Sitting in my office, glancing about for inspiration, my eyes lighted on the *Jeanie Johnston* literature, which I had never consigned to a file-- perhaps because it was an unresolved issue in my mind and I wasn't comfortable with the notion of closing it up in the file cabinet.

As I browsed through it and reread the exchange of letters from earlier in the year, a wild notion began to take root.

Wouldn't this be the ultimate millennium experience? It was sail all the way, crossing the Atlantic on a square-rigged ship. It would also be a uniquely appropriate way to honor Joanna O'Brien, by following her path across the Atlantic.

The thought began to dazzle. The adrenalin was flowing now, and I got up and paced about the office. I could virtually feel the gears of fate shifting into alignment and found myself wondering why I hadn't come to this conclusion sooner.

It was time, at the dawn of the millennium, for some notable venture, while I still had time and health, something I could call the adventure of a lifetime.

Why not?

"I'll tell you why not," said a little voice. "Because you're too old."

I knew that voice. I'd heard it before. It was Fogeyman, who, with all the stratagems at his disposal, always tries to make you feel as old as he can.

"What do you mean too old?" I said. "Sir Francis Chichester was an old man when he made his solo circumnavigation. So was Captain Joshua Slocum, the first man to sail alone around the world and write a classic book about it."

FM: "Come on, friend. Those guys were in their 60s when they did those things. You're approaching 80."

Me: "All right, smarty. How about George Bush's skydiving and John Glenn's return to space?"

FM: "Those were quick publicity shots. You're contemplating a long voyage. That takes staying power."

Me: "So what could happen?"

FM: "Anything, at your age. Heart attack, stroke, broken hip. You name it."

Me: "So? There'll be a doctor on the ship."

FM: "But no hospital, no intensive care facility."

I'd had enough of this. Fogeyman was using scare tactics.

"That's the politics of fear," I said, vaguely aware that I was drawing a phrase from the political arena.

11

FM: "But it could happen."

Me: "A lot of things could happen. I might die on the ship and be buried at sea. And that would be a great way to go!"

There was no answer. I listened into the silence for a while and finally concluded that I had bested Fogeyman on the ultimate question. He couldn't top that one.

In the months that followed, I never heard his voice again.

Next morning, I told Marie about my plan.

Marie had shown an adventurous streak herself, coming out of her routine life when we were married six years earlier to accompany me on walking tours along the trails and over the hills of England, Wales, Scotland, the American southwest and, most recently, Ireland.

It was in Ireland, finally, where she concluded she'd had enough. Out in the middle of a boggy wilderness, she caught her foot on a rock and fell, hitting her forehead on another rock. She got up quickly, and we determined she had no broken bones, but in the days that followed she developed a black eye so spectacular that our fellow walkers suggested I wear a sign around my neck saying "No, I don't beat my wife."

"I think I've had enough walking trips," Marie told me later, and I understood. She was, after all, 76, an age when most women would long since have consigned their hiking boots to the attic.

But she had no desire to curb my appetite for adventure. She listened intently while I related the conversation with Fogeyman. Then she leaned across the table, her chin in her hands, and looked me squarely in the eyes.

"It's the adventure of a lifetime. Go for it, Honey!"

I woke up the next morning full of fear. It had been eight or nine months since I'd received the letter from Ireland, and though there was not yet a captain at that time, he was to have been chosen in May, and he in turn would select the crew. It was now December.

Was I too late? The crew must have been selected-- from

12

hundreds of applications, I was sure-- by now, and the ship was scheduled to sail the following April-- only four months away. I'd have to make some special approach.

I carefully crafted a letter to the Captain. "I am a retired editor and writer," I said, "and a sailor as well. I would like to sail with the *Jeanie Johnston* on her April voyage and write her story for American media." I had very little to back that promise. "As a member of the Coast Guard Auxiliary," I said, "I would alert and arouse thousands of Auxiliarists to anticipate the *Jeanie Johnston*'s coming and turn out to greet her when she arrives." I had no idea how I would do that, but I was desperate.

The letter was mailed on December 19. We spent the millennium eve quietly, toasting each other with champagne and talking about the changes that were overtaking the world. And I hoped that out there somewhere in the night a great adventure might be shaping up for me.

CHAPTER 2
A Late-in-Life Sailor

The letter from Ireland was dated January 5, 2000, and it arrived as we were still trying to force ourselves to write the unfamiliar numerals, 2-0-0-0. There was something unreal about those numbers. For one thing, they had come too fast.

It has been said that time goes faster as one grows older. It's easy to dismiss that as a cliché, but hard to deny the reality of it. Let's say you live to be 90. At age 20, you have 70 years left, and a year goes by at the rate of 1/70th of your remaining life. At age 80, a year accounts for 1/10th of it. With 1/10th of your life crowded into one year, time goes a lot faster. Life, in other words, becomes more precious.

I had never thought I would live to see the millennium. In all my researches into family history, I had found no male Kindre who lived past age 70. Granted, age 70 in, say, 1850, was more noteworthy than age 70 today. Still, I had always pictured the year 2000, with its bright hopes, along with its burgeoning problems of a crowded planet, as an era beyond my lifetime. As the millennium approached, I began to sense, cautiously, and with no small sense of wonder, that I might indeed see it. Now I was not only in it; I had the audacity to plan a world-class adventure in celebration of it.

Would that grand adventure become a reality? The letter, from Ann Martin, the *Jeanie Johnston*'s marketing executive, burnished the possibility just a little.

The ship, she said, would carry 12 fee-paying passengers. "The 12 passages are the only positions available for the trans-atlantic voyage," she wrote. "They have not as of yet been allocated but there is significant demand. Capt. Forwood will choose his crew and passengers. If you are interested in taking one of these passages, please forward me details of your sailing experience."

There were a few subtle anomalies here. We had talked of "crew" positions. Now the only spots available were for "passengers." Being a passenger didn't promise to be as memorable as being a crew member; however, it still had merit. But why would a passenger need to be chosen on the basis of sailing experience?

I couldn't answer that, but I knew that whether I was to be called a passenger or a crew member, I wanted to be on the ship. So I began to write a resume of my sailing experience.

Actually, it had begun rather late in life. I was 48, in the midst of a New York career. Inez, my late wife, and I were sitting on the terrace of a resort hotel in St. Croix, sipping margaritas, when we noticed a sailboat leisurely drifting by in a light wind. There was something about the calm, sunny air; the relaxation of the cocktail hour and the vision of a boat with nowhere special to go just ghosting along in the golden light that struck a deep chord. "That's what I want to do," I said. "I'm going to take sailing lessons."

We were barely back from that St. Croix vacation when I signed up for offshore sailing lessons, and within a month had bought my first boat-- a 22-foot plywood sloop with a centerboard and sitting headroom in the cabin. Inez looked at it in the boatyard and said dryly, "Where will you ever find the time to work on a boat like that?"

I didn't know it then, but I was embarked on a dream that

couldn't last. While it did, though, it was delirious joy. We sailed every weekend, joined a yacht club, and in a year or two were ready for a larger boat.

"If you could buy any boat you wanted," I asked Ted, an old sea dog at the yacht club, "what would it be?" Ted had been sailing since he could walk. He answered without hesitation, "Either an Allied Sea Wind II ketch or a Tartan 30 sloop."

Inez and I sought them both out at the boat shows. We fell in love with the Sea Wind but it was far beyond our means. We bought a Tartan 30 and quickly learned to love it too, but then the dream began to thin out. My career was becoming more demanding, and after two years we took stock and realized we were sailing the boat only about half a dozen times during the summer, and we had never done anything but day sailing. In the end, it made no sense to keep the boat, and we reluctantly sold it.

For 20 years thereafter, there was no boat in our family. By 1991, I was ready to retire, and the prospect of sailing might have become reality again, but a year later Inez was diagnosed with cancer. When it reached the incurable stage, she elected to die at home with dignity. She left me quietly on a May afternoon, just four days past her 72nd birthday and seven months short of our 48th anniversary. The hospice nurse and social worker who were helping me tried to be comforting, and then, assured that I was in control, they left.

For two days, I was numb. Then I saw a great pit of emptiness opening up before me, and I knew I would be swallowed alive if I didn't take action. I willed myself to get busy, grasping first at the legal details-- the will, insurance, Social Security, credit cards. In a frenzy of gardening, I planted the beds of red salvia and pink begonias she had always loved. I drove to southern Ontario with our son to check some clues in an ancestral search for my grandfather's side of the family. It was a trip I had long thought about, and now it gave a semblance of purpose to my frantic nomadism, though in reality I knew I was simply running.

Back home again, the empty house was a shock. From the moment I opened the door, the rooms were full of her presence and the pain of her loss. My manufactured busyness was running down, and I knew I had to focus on something if I wanted to keep going. The simple fact was that Inez had been my life. Now my life was gone. Without it, I seemed to face two choices: either stop living or create a new life for myself.

What kind of new life would keep me busy enough to rise above the pain? Something that demanded commitment, that was physical and involved the emotions, something I could throw myself into with at least a show of enthusiasm?

The answer came quickly: a boat. And no sooner had the word "boat" risen to the surface than it was followed by "Allied Seawind II."

All the poignancy of that lost and almost-forgotten dream now came back to me. I quickly searched the classified ads in boating magazines and found four Seawind II's for sale-- one in Virginia, one in Maryland, one in Massachusetts and one in Buffalo, New York. The boat had not been built since 1980, so all would be in one state or another of secondhandedness.

I pulled out maps, began to check locations. A moment later, I backed away. This was a crazy idea. No one my age, in his right mind, should be buying a boat. A friend, the same age as I, was in the process of selling his boat. Why? Because he was an old man.

For a week, I blew hot and cold about the boat. Then I decided there was no harm in getting more information. I called two brokers, had them fax me spec sheets and began to assemble their data. By the time I decided to go out to dinner, I had a pile of notes and a modest amount of momentum going.

Returning a couple of hours later, I had barely closed the door behind me when I stopped in shock.

One of the fixtures of the vestibule, hanging on the wall next to the coat closet, was an enlarged color photo of a ketch under full sail. I had shot the photo one day just before sunset and al-

17

ways liked it because the brilliant white of the sails was in startling contrast to the darkening landscape behind them.

The picture had fallen from the wall and was wedged between the adjoining wall and a nearby chest of drawers.

My heart was pounding. Was this a message from that intersection of time and eternity? I was sure that Inez, wherever she was, was communicating with me. She was saying "Go for it!" It was all the impetus I needed.

I was on the phone the following day, and a few days later I was in Buffalo. The Seawind II that was for sale there was 17 years old, and it sounded the most promising of the lot simply because it had been used in a fresh water environment and therefore its rigging would have been less subject to corrosion.

The boat, when I first saw it, was in its cradle in the yard. Its graceful lines were vaguely familiar but it had a derelict look about it. The name on its transom was *"Four Winds."*

"The owner never put it in the water this season, or last season either," said the marina manager. No wonder it looked forlorn. It had been sitting there in the yard for a year and a half.

The cockpit looked like Dracula's castle. Festoons of giant cobwebs hung from the mizzen mast and the shrouds, covered the hatch and choked the wheel in their filmy grip. There was no place to sit down, and every step had to be preceded by a sweep of the hand to clear a path. Spiders scurried everywhere.

"He has to sell it," said the manager, "or at least his family is telling him he has to. You see, he's in the early stages of Alzheimer's, and it's difficult for him to make decisions."

I hoped my expression didn't reveal my inner thoughts. My God, the owner must be as old as I am. But he was getting out, while I was only starting.

Nevertheless, I had a good feeling about this boat. I had many questions, and we spent a half hour or so going over them. At the end, I concluded, and the manager agreed, that while the owner had done very little to augment the boat's capabilities, he had treated it gently and it was basically in good con-

18

dition.

I sat on one of the bunks, breathed in the scent of the teak, basked in the neglected but cozy interior and finally made the manager an offer. He thought my figure was reasonable and said he would convey it to the owner.

Within two weeks, I was back in Buffalo, had signed the necessary papers and was the new owner of *Four Winds*. As a boat owner, I now had a clear set of priorities. First rechristen the boat with a name of my own choice. Second, get her in the water. And third, go sailing.

It would be several days before she arrived in New Jersey, but I had already decided on a name. I eliminated the traditional names of stars and seabirds as too routine. I thought of naming her for Inez, but I didn't believe Inez would be conformable having a boat named for her. What name would signify my new life? The answer, when it came, was just right: "*Second Wind.*" It was a proper sailboat name and it also succinctly described my late-in-life venture onto the seas.

In mid-August, the tractor with its flatbed trailer pulled into the Brielle Marine Basin, and the boat was unloaded. On that day, the focus of my life changed. My activities, attention and plans began to revolve around the boatyard. It became my place of work and pleasure. I arrived in the morning, spent much of the day there, and often, in the evening, or after returning from a beach walk, I would stop by just to look at my boat and ponder what lay in the future for the two of us.

When the fear came that I was no match for her, or that it was too late in life to embark on this new course, I would go home and reread-- perhaps for the hundredth time-- one of my favorite poems, Tennyson's *Ulysses*, especially the lines in which the aging king tells his mariners,

> *"You and I are old;*
> *Old age hath yet his honor and his toil.*
> *Death closes all; but something ere the end,*

Some work of noble note, may yet be done...
'Tis not too late to seek a newer world,
Push off, and sitting well in order smite
The sounding furrows; for my purpose holds
To sail beyond the sunset, and the baths
Of all the western stars, until I die....
To strive, to seek, to find, and not to yield."

What I feared, more than the dangers of the sea, was the life I saw being lived by many men my age. I would see them in restaurants, alone, slouching and listless. Were their thoughts, I wondered, as dull as their eyes? Did they go home and spend the rest of the day watching television? What were their plans for the future?

The dominant theme of my immediate future was the need to get to work. The deck was a dirty mess. I started from the bow and worked my way back, scrubbing with soap and bleach. The temperature was in the 90s, and before long the sweat was pouring from me. But the results were so pleasing I didn't notice the discomfort.

I looked at my watch. "If I work another three-quarters of an hour, I can finish this and knock off for lunch," I told myself. Almost immediately, a voice in my head said "Stop now."

Suddenly, I realized how close to exhaustion I was. At lunch, I thought over what had just happened. Again, I had been influenced benignly by some power outside myself. Another little nudge. Since Inez died, there seemed to be more of them, and I wondered if I had a new advocate before whatever court there was in the realm of the infinite. I was attuned now to the little nudges, and they seemed invariably to be elements in some positive protective force.

Over the next few days, I snuffed out hundreds of spiders and their webs, waxed the topsides and oiled the teak. The sails and rigging were inspected and the engine checked and tuned. The artist who specialized in boat lettering asked me what style I wanted, and I decided on green with gold outlining. Within a couple of hours, *Four Winds* was magically transformed into *Second Wind*.

What a difference a name makes. Now she was really mine. I found myself stopping at the boatyard at odd times, early in the morning or late in the evening, just to look at the transom with its handsome new lettering and feel the emotions of pride and hope and the tingle of adventure yet to come.

Now there was just one more thing to be done before I sailed.

Sitting on the gallery at the back of my desk at home was a gargoyle, a little stoneware figure with a monster's head and a human body, folded wings, arms crossed at the wrists and legs crossed at the ankles. It had been Inez's final gift to me. She was lying on the sofa the day the package arrived, too weak to move about. When I opened it, she saw my puzzled look and smiled.

"It's to remind you of me when I'm gone," she said. "Keep it somewhere where it can stand guard for you."

There was no need to say anything more. Inez and I both knew that the function of gargoyles in medieval architecture was to keep evil spirits away. After she died, I kept it on my desk, and when I was distressed, I would stroke the little figure's feet and murmur, "No evil spirits." In time the gargoyle became a talisman of hope.

Now I knew that its proper place was aboard *Second Wind*. I built a small shelf for it to sit on and installed it on the edge of a bulkhead between the galley and the main cabin.

In the months that followed, *Second Wind* restored my soul. I found new friends-- retirees like myself-- and together we took her out on the ocean, sailed up and down the coast, and soon were ready for slightly longer passages. Tony Esposito, Carl Olbrich and I sailed on a weekend to Fire Island Inlet on the south coast of Long Island, and on another weekend Tony and I took *Second Wind* up the New Jersey coast and inside

Sandy Hook to a marina at Atlantic Highlands. The sun, the wind, the salt air and the comradeship were the tonic I needed, and *Second Wind* proved to be steady, seaworthy and a joy to handle. I was learning to live with my grief and still have a life.

Now I began to plan the next step-- a long voyage, perhaps to Florida or even farther, to the Caribbean. It would take a higher level of experience, the willingness to adventure, and the availability and commitment of companions who were like-minded. At least two of my crew members seemed up to it, and we started thinking seriously about a cruise down the Intracoastal Waterway to Florida.

Meanwhile, I was beginning to feel strong enough to reach out to relatives I hadn't seen in years. One of them was my first cousin Marie, whom I had last been in touch with some 20 years earlier. She was shocked when she answered the phone: "Tom, I didn't think I'd ever hear from you again."

I had many questions about the family. I learned that Marie had been a widow for 12 years. Her daughter Nancy was in her 30s and had a two-and-a-half-year-old daughter of her own. We agreed to meet soon.

Families had once bored me. Now I hungered for them. Where once I had fled, I now wanted to belong. Inez and I had built a nest for ourselves and had effectively shut out the world. For the survivor, assuming one of us would outlive the other, that posed the challenge of starting a new life, building new connections, at a time, late in life, when it would not be easy to do that. But at least I had started.

My ties to Marie were especially strong. Our maternal grandparents had a spacious house, and both my mother and her sister (Marie's mother) had married and brought their husbands home to live until they had the opportunity and the means to set up their own households. Marie, her brother, who died in World War II, and I were born within a two-year period in that ancestral home and played together as siblings. In effect, we grew up together, and while no one else ever knew, least of all

22

Marie herself, I had been half in love with her when we were teenagers.

We were separated by college, World War II and marriage. Over the course of some 50 years, we probably had seen one another three or four times, usually at the funeral of a family member. Now we were about to meet again.

A few days later, I had a cordial and emotional visit with Marie. She was just as I had remembered her-- a bright, sunny disposition, a wonderful smile, and great fun to be with. On top of all that, we had mutual ties that went back quite literally to the beginning of our lives. We were soon having dinner together rather frequently.

Over a period of months, an idea-- absurd at first, but gradually becoming more acceptable-- kept recurring: Marie might become more than just my cousin. I knew she was fond of me, and the cousin connection hardly had any relevance at our ages. But would she be offended by my even suggesting the idea? I was afraid to ask, but the notion would not go away. I wrestled with it during a walking trip in England and came to a resolution while pacing a trail along the cliffs of Cornwall. I would ask Marie to marry me, and if she thought the idea was absurd, so be it.

It didn't take long, after my return, to find the right occasion. And to my happy surprise, Marie said "yes." Her 97-year-old mother, whom she had cared for, had died a few months earlier and her life had entered a new stage that required new decisions. She had worked as a college administrator for some 20 years, and it was time to retire. Our belated reunion was a timely catalyst that was soon to open the door to a new life for both of us.

The wedding was celebrated aboard a pennant-bedecked *Second Wind*, with the boat berthed in a corner slip in the marina and our guests seated on chairs arranged around the dock. When the ceremony ended, we embarked on a five-minute triumphal cruise, then returned and walked with our friends to a dockside restaurant for the wedding reception.

23

My plan to sail off to the islands had been short-circuited but not abandoned. About a month before the wedding, I had written to my sailing friends suggesting that two or three of them might take the boat to Florida without me. "Last year *Second Wind* sat idle in a winter-bound boatyard," I wrote. "This year she should be in her element and in use. If this plan is to work, the crew must seize the initiative. I am too busy and will not be part of the project in any case."

Two crew members, Carl Olbrich and Hank Malek, seized the initiative and set their departure date for October 8, the day after our wedding. At our reception, the heartiest toast, next to that for the bride and groom, was to the crew of *Second Wind.* Early the following morning, while Marie and I flew off to our Bermuda honeymoon, Carl and Hank were on their way down the New Jersey coast on the first leg of their 1,500-mile voyage.

The projected winter cruising didn't work out as planned. We went to Florida but spent much of our time fighting the flu rather than sailing. Then the boat virtually refused to move under power and it was only after hiring a diver that we discovered her propeller was totally encrusted with barnacles. These and other glitches reduced our grand scheme to a total of two day sails. But in the spring adventure was to flower at last in the way I had hoped it would.

Carl and his wife Gwynne boarded the boat in April and took her from her west coast dock through the St. Lucie Canal and up the east coast to Jacksonville, where Gwynne, a new grandmother, flew off to be with her daughter and new granddaughter. I flew to Jacksonville, joined Carl, and together we brought *Second Wind* up the Intracoastal Waterway. At Norfolk, Marie joined us and we three voyaged the rest of the way home.

It was an adventure never to be forgotten. From Jacksonville, we set a course for Georgetown, South Carolina, that put us well offshore. Two days and two nights out of sight of land provided a brief glimpse of what a real voyage is all about. We stood watch, kept lookout for commercial vessels that might run

24

us down and prayed for good weather (successfully, most of the time). Later, in the Carolinas, there were exciting stretches of jungle-like rivers with tangled vines overhead, a long reach through the Dismal Swamp Canal into Virginia, two accidental groundings and a day of 30-knot winds when we fought a following sea all the way across North Carolina's Albemarle Sound. I was aboard the boat for six weeks, Marie for three.

That, plus the Virgin Islands charter and an earlier one in the Greek Isles, was the sum total of my sailing experience. I had never single-handed across the ocean or raced to Block Island. I had never crewed a square-rigged ship; in fact, I had never been on a square-rigged ship. The details would hardly be of interest to Captain Forwood, so I distilled them into half a page, skipping quickly over the weak spots and putting the best possible face on what substance there was, and sent it off to Ireland.

Had I made a good decision, or was I out of my mind?

When I needed mental space and freedom from distractions, I usually went aboard *Second Wind*-- whether she was in the water or out-- and in the space of a few minutes meditation I invariably found some peaceful inner resolution.

Second Wind and I had an intimate relationship. In our early days together, when I was alone, I talked to her frequently. When I was aboard her, even at the dock, she seemed a sensate creature, always moving slightly, with little whisperings and murmerings about her hull. We were a team, and we had formed a pact, not known until now by anyone else.

If I depart this life first, *Second Wind* will bury me at sea. My will states that my ashes will be scattered from the boat while she is under sail with a friend at the wheel. If *Second Wind* becomes incapacitated first, through some catastrophic accident or other incident that renders her unsailable, I will not let her rot away in a boatyard but will tow her out to sea and open her sea cocks, giving her the dignity of a proper burial in the medium for which she was born.

It was midwinter now, and the boatyard was a frozen wasteland. *Second Wind* was up on her blocks, immobile and mute. I put up a ladder, clambered aboard, opened the hatch and went below. I knew I couldn't stay long; the cold was bone-numbing. All it took was a minute or two, though.

"What do you think, *Second Wind*?" I asked. The only audible answer was a metallic shudder as a blast of wind shivered her masts, but somehow I knew what was in her heart. It went something like this: "Anything is better than sitting unused in a boat yard; don't let it happen to you." There was wisdom in that thought.

And the gargoyle-- what did he think? Inscrutable as always, he stared straight ahead and gave not the slightest hint of a negative expression. If there were any evil spirits about, he'd handle them in his own way.

And that was good enough for me.

CHAPTER 3

The Battle of the Ages

"How old are you?" Captain Mike Forwood asked. It was February, 2000, and I was on the phone with the *Jeanie Johnston's* master. He had read my sailing resume and wanted more information.

"Well," I hesitated. "I know the ship's insurance covers people only up to age 69, and I'm older than that."

"Then you'll have to get your own insurance. So, then, how old are you?"

"I'm in my 70s," I ventured, not wanting to squelch my chances before he'd even met me or had any idea about my capabilities.

"Not too high up in the 70s, I hope."

"I certainly hope not," I responded. In truth, I would be almost 79 when the ship was scheduled to sail in April. "Contact the *Guinness Book of World Records*," my son-in-law had suggested. "You might become the oldest man ever to cross the Atlantic on the crew of a square-rigged ship."

I definitely did not want this conversational turn to go any further. I was certain I could find a way to document my fitness for the voyage and place it in front of the captain in a persuasive way. If I were rejected out of hand at this point I might not have that opportunity. So I tried to deflect further talk of age by asking "What do I have to do next to apply for a crew position?"

"You'll need to fill out a berth application form and a medical questionnaire. We need to know more about you-- your age, next of kin, your general state of fitness, etc. There are things you must be able to do, you know. There's a sea survival course for the crew, and you'll have to be dunked in the water wearing an immersion suit."

Immersion suits had not been part of my experience, and I didn't look forward to being dunked, but I was prepared to do anything within reason to get a crew berth.

I sent off the two forms next day, along with a deposit for my fare. Fortunately, I could answer "No" to all major physical problems, but I finally had to reveal my age and I was worried about the outcome, so I devised a strategy of overkill. If I talked enough about fitness, he might assume I wasn't afraid of the subject and was likely, therefore, to be reasonably fit. Whether this trick had any bearing on my case, I'll never know, but here is the kind of rhetoric I threw at him:

"In choosing your passengers and crew and providing for their health at sea, I am sure you will have in mind the 'healthy' record of the original *Jeanie Johnston* and take every precaution to avoid accidents or illnesses. I am in excellent health and would be glad to submit a physician's certificate to that effect.

"But you may want all passengers and crew (I still didn't know whether I was to be a passenger or a crew member) to take a physical examination given by a physician of your choice, and I would have no objection to that.

"I am accustomed to working out every other day on cardiovascular and strength machines at a fitness center. I can't imagine that the ship would have room for a fully fitted-out workout center, but I wonder if you have made provision for some form of exercise to keep your passengers fit."

What a stilted mouthful of words! The time would come when I would wish I hadn't written them, but I was desperate to get past this age barrier. I didn't feel decrepit, and I didn't think it was fair to be disqualified solely on the basis of the calendar.

A week later, we talked again.

"Well, you sound fit enough," the Captain began, "but because of your age I'll definitely need a letter from your doctor--and you'll have to get your own insurance. Our insurers consider this voyage a dangerous event, not a holiday cruise, and that's why they've picked age 69 as the top limit for individuals they can cover under the ship's blanket policy."

I thanked him and set to work. First I called Bob, a Coast Guard Auxiliary friend who works for a major insurance company. Bob looked into it and told me to call Barbara at an agency he thought could help. Barbara forwarded my requirements to her commercial department and called back a day later to say they had never put together a package like the one I needed and that it was beyond the scope of their work.

I can't say I was surprised. Commercial agencies don't get too many calls from people who are about to make a transatlantic crossing on a square-rigged ship and need life, disability and liability insurance to match the standards set by the ship's project management.

"Why don't you try agencies that are marine-oriented?" suggested one of the agents I talked to. That sounded like a good idea. I started with Boat U.S., the boat owners association, and they gave me the names of three agencies. One of them was Blue Water Insurance, another was World Marine. Now, I thought, I'm in the right camp. But no, they mostly insured tour operators and charter fleets in a limited area such as the Virgin Islands. As for an Atlantic crossing, no way.

"Your best bet lies somewhere in Ireland or in London," one of them offered. "Why don't you talk to the broker who's assembling the underwriters for the ship's own insurance?"

That's when I became acquainted with Ronnie Dolan, the broker in Waterford, Ireland, who had set that 69-year-old limit for the *Jeanie Johnston* voyage. Why I should expect any help from him, I didn't know, but who else was there?

Ronnie came on the phone with a voice full of that lilt that the rest of the world associates with the quintessential Irishman. Listen to it for a minute or two, regardless of what he's saying, and behold! the world is a better and brighter place, full of joy, zest and passion.

"So you want to be on that ship, do you? And at your age yet! What will you do when they want you to go to the top of the mast? You think you can do that, do you?"

I detected a hint of a lilt in my own voice as I responded. I find the Irish lilt a very attractive habit of speech and tend to fall into it myself when with Irish speakers. But I must be careful lest they think I am mocking them, so I held myself in check. I wanted to avoid at all cost making a bad impression on this man who might hold my fate as a *Jeanie Johnston* crew member in the palm of his hand.

I told him what I had written to Captain Forwood and described my physical condition and my exercise regimen. "Well, send me the particulars," he said. "I can't guarantee anything, but we'll see what we can do."

I wrote immediately, enclosing a copy of the sailing credentials and the medical questionnaire I had already given to Captain Forwood. "As for my age," I said, "I can assure you that I have no disabilities, no medical problems, no allergies, nothing that will affect my ability to fully participate in the voyage. On my own boat, whose mast rises 50 feet, I am the only one who goes to the top in a bosun's chair when needed, while other crew members claim dizziness or fear of heights." (That was true enough.) "My doctor says I have a physique that a man of 60 would be proud to have." (A bit of hyperbole. My doctor had said I was in good shape, though he'd never compared me with a 60-year-old. But I thought if push came to shove, I might be able to get him to say it. I had to impress Ronnie Dolan.)

"Every other day," I told him, "I work out at a fitness center- - 45 minutes of cardiovascular exercise on treadmills, rowing machines and a Stairmaster, followed by an hour of strength training to build muscle in arms, legs, back, abdomen, etc. If you need letters from my doctor or the health training specialists at the fitness center, I'll be glad to send them."

Then, to clinch things, I called my doctor and asked him to arrange for an exercise stress test. I wanted to provide Ronnie Dolan with every possible proof that I wasn't a decadent old man. I passed the test handily, thanks, I'm sure, to my regular 15-minute workouts on the Stairmaster, which told me at the conclusion of each exercise period that I had done the equivalent of climbing 56 flights of stairs.

I then asked Dr. Micallef to write a letter reporting the results of the test and attesting to my good health generally. The doctor came through for me with a couple of sentences that couldn't have been better: "I consider Mr. Kindre an excellent candidate for the trip he is contemplating. If you have any questions, feel free to call me."

Now I had some ammunition, and I sent it off in high spirits to both Ronnie Dolan and Captain Forwood. Thank God for the workout program, I thought, and in the next breath I thanked Marie. I'd never have seen the Life Fitness Center if it hadn't been for her. I'm too lazy to have thought of it for myself.

At the time of our marriage, Marie had just emerged from a period of her life when she had been under great stress, holding a professional job while caring for her 97-year old bedridden mother. I insisted that she needed a program to build back her energy. When she signed up for the fitness program, I did too, and it was one of the best decisions I've ever made.

We found, remarkably, that even in our mid- to late 70s, we could still build muscle, gaining energy and stamina in the process. But it wasn't always easy to gather the will to do it. There were mornings when I woke up, rolled over and said "I sure don't feel like exercising today." But Marie would be likely to say "I don't either. So let's go," and off we would go to our tri-weekly session.

Approaching 80, we learned, you're likely to lose 50 percent of your muscle mass if you fail to exercise. Over three years or so, we had actually gained muscle-- not much, but enough to see. "You'll never look like one of those photos in the muscle magazines," said Dr. Micallef, "but you're doing fine."

I was still hauling halyards and grinding winches aboard *Second Wind*, and even clambering around on the foredeck when necessary. Those tasks take some strength and agility. I had trouble, though, when it came to folding up my bones and contorting my body into some cramped corner of the engine compartment. I discovered this problem early on in my experience with *Second Wind*.

One day I had to go down into one of the cockpit lockers to access an engine control. It's a narrow, tight space that requires some gymnastics, but I had seen an engine mechanic do it, and he must have been 6 feet 5 at least, far taller than I. What I didn't reckon with was the fact that he was also much younger. I got my body twisted into a position where I could reach the controls and perform the task I had to, and then, to my consternation, I couldn't untangle my legs and make my way out.

There I was, down in the locker, invisible to anyone outside and unable to help myself. I considered my options. I could stay there until someone came along, or I could call for help. If I did that, one of the boatyard crew would probably have heard me and come to the rescue. But the aftermath was too much to contemplate. They'd all be laughing for weeks at the old man who was so weak and cramped up that he couldn't get out of his own boat.

At that point, I saw the humor in the situation and began to laugh. Laughter does something salubrious to the brain-- causes it to produce endorphins, I believe-- and in no time I found I could untie my knotted legs and get up into the daylight. After that, I gave up going into tight compartments. I had sailing companions, after all, who were younger and more agile, and I deferred to them when the need arose.

Aside from that problem, though, I felt stronger approaching 80 than I had at 73 or 74, before we began our fitness program. Moreover, the dedicated health professionals at the fitness center had saved me from a couple of situations that might have been physical disasters.

Old backs are invariably troublesome, and mine is no exception. X-rays have shown traces of arthritis up and down the spinal column, resulting in low-level pain part of the time and an inherent weariness at other times. Those were the easy times. The hard times were when I made a foolish move, or attempted an awkward lift, and suddenly two or three disks would be out of kilter, with pain shooting down the sciatic nerves into my legs. If it was bad enough, I'd visit my chiropractor. But I needed to make those visits less frequently because of Carolan.

Carolan leads a "Back Attack" class at the fitness center. The hours we spend with her twice a week had taught me how to extract the most usefulness from an aging back and avoid the carelessness to which we are all prone as we forget that we are no longer the men-- or women-- we once were.

Shortly after I became interested in the *Jeanie Johnston* voyage, I had a back episode that threatened to lay me low. A chiropractic treatment helped but not enough. I asked Carolan if it was safe for me to take part in her exercise class

She looked at me askance. "Tom, that's what this class is all about. It can't hurt your back; it can only help." I trusted her. It was just that I thought I shouldn't be doing all that moving around with a back that still had some recovering to do. A few minutes into the session, though, I began to feel a warm glow in the areas where the pain still lingered. Carolan's magic is compounded of yoga, proper breathing, posture control and the "Pilates" technique, a regimen that combines stretching and strengthening routines designed to work the entire body. And she somehow makes it all palatable with a constant line of patter.

"All right, just five more times now. . .don't give up. . .you know I love you. . .now raise that arm toward the ceiling. . .I wouldn't do anything to hurt you. . .stretch forward as far as you can. . .make that hamstring sing. . .where are those belly buttons?. . .they're pulled in tight. . .feet firmly planted, hips over feet, belly button in, chest out, shoulders down. . .find that neutral posture. . .you can do it, I know you can."

Sometimes it hurt, but it always felt good when it was over. And it made us conscious of our posture. The idea was to isolate and work muscles you didn't know you had. Most of us have unbalanced bodies, Carolan explained, because we tend to overdevelop the major muscle groups, leading to poor posture and spinal misalignment. So we worked at strengthening the abdominal muscles and the muscles around the spine to take pressure off the back.

"You're my dream girl," I told her. "Your face appears in my dreams, and you're saying over and over, 'pull that belly button in.' And even in my dreams, I do."

Since the advent of the *Jeanie Johnston*, the fitness center had taken on certain aspects of a war room. It had become the headquarters of my campaign to hold off the ravages of age, and its staff members were my staff officers, helping me develop a strategic plan.

Captain Forwood wanted able-bodied seamen, not out-of-shape old men, so I knew if I really wanted to do this crazy voyage, it was up to me to whip my aged body into shape and try to keep it that way. Now, if I missed a workout session, my conscience told me I was reducing my chances of getting that crew slot. If I longed to turn over and go back to sleep, I conjured up a picture of salt spray and white sails snapping in the wind, and the vision was often as instantly energizing as a cup of coffee. If it was a low-energy day and I was tempted to cut a session short, I pictured the bosun's mate ordering out the watch-- including me-- and assigning their stations.

"Got to get those muscles in shape to climb the ratlines!" was a greeting I frequently got from friends at Life Fitness. Or "It's a long way to the top of the mast. Are you ready for that?" Or "If you really expect to climb that rigging, you'd better do double duty here."

Fred and Rich and Ed especially went out of their way to offer helpful advice. "There's no need to worry about sharks," they assured me. "If you fall from the top of the mast in the North Atlantic, hypothermia will do you in long before the sharks can get to you."

While I was still waiting to hear from Ronnie Dolan, a semi-disaster struck. I'd been aware of a pain in my shoulder but had ignored it, hoping it would go away. It didn't; it got worse. This was food for panic. I couldn't haul lines or climb aloft with a painful shoulder. An X-ray showed a rotator cuff problem. There was hardly any cartilage left, said the orthopedist I consulted, and there were only two things to do: cortisone shots, which would give only temporary relief; or surgery. I didn't fancy either.

At our next fitness session, I told Jackie, the manager, about my problem. Jackie is a knockout of a woman, a real health pro, with better musculature than I could ever attain and a friendly but laid-back manner. I had watched her one day as she listened to a sad story told by an elderly woman who obviously needed someone to talk to. Her expression was fully attentive, and her patience and empathy were obvious as she waved away an assistant intent on interrupting.

Jackie led me straight to the cable column, a machine on which you pull cables with weights attached. "There are three muscles that control the rotator cuff," she said, and proceeded to demonstrate exercises for two of them. The third I would exercise with a free weight. "But the doctor told me the cartilage was gone," I reminded her. "Just do it," she smiled.

Within two or three sessions, the pain was gone. I made the exercises a part of my regular regimen, and the shoulder has been in operable condition ever since.

Carolan, Jackie, Cheryl, Kelly, Pat and all the others...they walk in beauty, every one of them. Without their warmth, their caring help and their personal interest, I'd never have been able to hold my old body together and wouldn't even have considered trying to gain a crew slot on the *Jeanie Johnston*.

By now, I thought, there had been time for Ronnie Dolan to receive my letter and act on it, if he were going to, so I called Waterford.

"Sure, and you're just a minor part of my problem," he told me. "There are four different underwriters I'm working with, and many points to be negotiated. But (*almost as an after-thought*) I sent your letter to them, and one has replied. He says you must be more fit than Lyn Christie, and he'll put you in as part of the ship's package. I'm waiting to hear from the three others, and anything could happen. So keep your hopes up, but don't let them get too high."

I didn't know whether this was good news or bad. I wasn't out of it yet, and with one underwriter at least I seemed to have broken the age barrier. As to who Lyn Christie was, I could only guess he was some Irish athlete or other. But Captain Forwood still seemed leery about the age issue, and I felt I needed more ammunition to convince both him and the insurers that I was healthy enough to be a crew member, and that age shouldn't be a factor in the decision.

What I ought to have was some dramatic ace in the hole that I could use if and when needed to defuse the age problem. Former Senator and astronaut John Glenn had only recently returned to space at age 77, and the whole world knew about his successful flight. I knew he had been chairman of the Senate's Special Committee on Aging and had faced the age issue himself in numerous interviews. Suppose I could get him to write a letter for me decrying the criterion of age alone as a determinant in space flights, ocean voyages or any other ventures? He was an international hero, and his intervention might impress the *Jeanie Johnston* people.

I didn't know Senator Glenn, but a query to the webmaster of the Senate brought me the address and phone number of his of-

36

fice at Ohio State University, where he had made his headquarters since retiring from the Senate. I began to compose a letter to him.

Meanwhile, another thought was taking shape. We all know a picture is worth a thousand words, and I couldn't imagine why this possibility hadn't occurred to me earlier. Captain Forwood and Ronnie Dolan had both talked with me on the phone, and they had read my credentials, but they had never seen me. What picture had they formed of me? Did they automatically expect a 79-year-old man to look bent, wrinkled and feeble? Would my appearance be out of keeping with that of a sturdy-looking crew?

I grabbed a camera and asked Marie to take some pictures. It was early March and still quite cold, but I felt an outdoor shot would be best. I stripped to a pair of shorts and struck an aggressive pose while she took several photos. I got them developed the same day and mailed prints the next day to both Captain Forwood and Ronnie Dolan.

A few days later, a letter arrived from Captain Forwood. "Thank you for sending the berth application form and the medical questionnaire, as well as your deposit," it said "The latter has secured for you a position as one of the supernumerary crew members of the ship, subject to your obtaining suitable insurance coverage. The voyage from Tralee to Washington, DC is expected to take about five weeks and you will be asked to join several days in advance of the ship sailing for training, including a statutory sea survival course. The current sailing date is May 7, but this may change. You will be informed of any date change."

One down and one to go. I took this to mean that I had been accepted by Captain Forwood as a member of his crew, and that I now had to target my efforts on Ronnie Dolan and the insurance coverage. The fact that one of the four underwriters had accepted me on the basis of the information I'd sent was a good sign. And by now Ronnie would have in hand the photos of me shivering in the backyard. It had been a week since I'd talked to him and time to call again.

"Well, you look to me as though you'd have no trouble climbing up that mast," he began, and I thanked God for inspiring me to send the photos. "There are some delays in getting the whole package together, and some complications in the coverage-- nothing to do with you-- but things are moving along. Oh, and by the way, a second underwriter has agreed to include you in the ship's coverage."

That was what I wanted to hear. "Does that mean I'm in?"

"The *Jeanie Johnston* management still has to make some choices among insurance options, but I'd say you're solidly aboard now. You're part of the package, so however they make their final decision, when they make it the tide will come in and all the boats will rise together."

"I take it I'll be one of those boats."

"You will be, indeed."

Captain Forwood was in the US when I called, making port arrangements. Michael O'Carroll, the chief engineer, congratulated me and welcomed me to the crew. But he had some bad news, too-- foreshadowed by the uncertainty expressed in the Captain's last letter. The problems of building a 19th century ship in the 21st century were now coming into focus. First, there was the wood-- just the right cuts of Irish oak for her frames and Austrian larch for her planking. One wood shipment wasn't the best, so it was rejected. That meant going back to the woods, searching for and cutting new wood.

Then there was the problem of the shipwrights. There are only so many left in the world who know the old techniques, and they had to be sought out and induced to come to Ireland, where they had been supervising and teaching young trainees from several nations. But the shipwright/superintendents couldn't stay forever, and some had left, necessitating a worldwide quest for others to take their places.

The upshot of all this, said Michael, was delay. The ship

wouldn't sail before May 27, and even that date was uncertain. He suggested I check back every couple of weeks.

The delay didn't bother me greatly, and I was in a celebratory mood as Marie and I made arrangements to fly to St. Vincent in the Windward Islands with Nancy and Brooks for another bareboat charter-- this one a run down the Grenadines to Grenada.

We picked up our chartered Beneteau 400 sloop and headed south in a glorious wind that sent us boiling along to Bequia, yachting crossroads of the Caribbean, and Mustique, home to Princess Margaret and Mick Jagger.

On Mayreau, largely uninhabited, we walked over a mountain trail to a restaurant and returned in the dark, picking our way down the mountain by flashlight. In the Tobago Cays, we bought lobsters from a bumboat, grilled them on a deserted beach and ate to the accompaniment of moonlight, rum and a Jimmy Buffett CD.

In Grenada, we took a day-long safari tour of the island, with its lush nutmeg groves and rare flowering trees. Half way through, our guide said "I know of a little out-of-the-way place where we could get a real island lunch." Adventurers all, we agreed. It was indeed a tiny hole-in-the-wall with not a tourist in sight. Two of us had beef stew, and while I was waiting to pay the bill I noticed, on a side table, a book entitled *A Manual for Dissecting the Dog* that left us wondering what we had eaten.

But a gala event later that day made up for it. We were invited to a party at the waterfront home of my old friend Royston Hopkin, owner of the Spice Island Inn and former head of the Caribbean Tourist Association.

Royston, who had known me for some years, was intrigued with my *Jeanie Johnston* venture and sought to pooh-pooh the age issue. "John Glenn just went back into space," he offered, "so why shouldn't you sail the Atlantic?"

I didn't tell him I had fingered the astronaut as a possible aide if there was to be a battle over age discrimination.

As it turned out, I didn't need him.

CHAPTER 4
Square Rigger Hubris

"I hope the Captain doesn't make us run."

I set down the book I'd been reading. These were jubilant days now that I'd been accepted as a crew member on the *Jeanie Johnston*. I was in square-rigger heaven, and I'd been reading about the history of square-rigged ships. In the early 19th Century British Navy, when the watch was mustered, all hands went to their posts on the run. The upper yardmen, who worked high up among the topgallants and royals, were supposed to get to their stations at the same time as everyone else. It looked more orderly that way. But it turned out to be a health hazard. By mid-century, it was noted that upper yardmen were more susceptible to heart trouble than others. So the Admiralty ordered a "breather"--a five-minute head start-- to make the trip aloft less strenuous.

Captain Forwood didn't look like a tyrant in the pictures I'd seen of him, and he sounded cordial when I talked to him on the phone. I could only hope he wasn't committed to an orderly ship above all else.

In the old days, the forecastlemen, who worked the headsails and cleared away and secured the anchors, were the biggest, strongest men on the ship. I was sure others would be assigned to that job. The smallest men and boys worked the royal yards, at the very top. That seemed an appropriate task for the teenage trainees who would be aboard the ship.

Digging more deeply into crew assignments, I found one I might like. John Harland, in *Seamanship in the Age of Sail,* says "Older, more experienced, but physically less active seamen were detailed as captains of the mast, in charge of handing out and belaying gear at the foot of the mast." The only problem with that was the "experienced"part. I had never been on a square-rigged ship, let alone chalked up any experience on one.

I asked a friend who was once a cadet on the sail training ship *Danmark* what it was like. He said the scariest part was when your duty took you to the top of the mainmast, and the ship was rolling. "One minute you were looking down at blue water off the port side," he said, "and the next you were suspended out over open water on the starboard side. There was a tiny little deck down below that looked like its only purpose was to serve as a fulcrum for your wild gyrations."

A tiny little deck? I had seen the *Danmark* when she was docked along the west wall of Baltimore's Inner Harbor during the Op Sail celebration. She appeared gargantuan-- all 263 feet of her. And what freeboard! She looked three stories high, at least.

By contrast, I had taken special note of two boats-- the topsail schooner *Pride of Baltimore* and the *Oosterschelde,* from Rotterdam, because both are about the size of the *Jeanie Johnston*-- some 125 feet in length, 26 feet or so in the beam and with fairly low freeboard. Wherever you went on deck, you'd be close to the water. It's a bit like the difference between a sports car and a truck. I've always said I like a car that sits me down close to the road because it's more fun to drive. I'd soon have my chance to see if I felt the same way about ships.

In the 19th century, when the watch came on deck, they had to "answer their stations." This constant drill was designed to make a seaman's duties so familiar to him that he could almost respond in his sleep. The lieutenant would call out a specific exercise, like "Shifting topmasts!" and each man would respond by describing what his action would be in response to that order. One might call out "Reeve fore top-tackle fall," and the next one, "Weather reef-tackle, fore tack and bowline." To today's sailors, those terms sound almost as obscure as if they were written in an extinct language.

By the middle of the 19th century, the positions where the ropes (sheets) controlling the sails were fastened on deck were standardized by international law, so, as David MacGregor says in *Square Rigged Sailing Ships*, "a German sailor shanghaied out of San Francisco aboard a British ship knew just where to go on deck to lay his hand on the main upper topsail halyard on being aroused from his drunken sleep as the ship was being towed to sea."

There were times, of course, when every sailor was happy to know that every other sailor knew by heart every word of the drill-- and knew exactly what to do when he heard it. When the cry, "Man overboard" rang out, there was precious little time in which to throw a life buoy, stop a square-rigged ship in its tracks, launch a boat and effect a rescue. The commands were precise, the order in which they were given was precise, and the response of every man on the watch had to be just as precise.

Here, thanks to Harland, is the exact sequence of orders in the process of heaving to for a rescue effort when a ship is sailing by the wind: "Hard down! Let go the life buoy! Silence fore and aft! (to avoid panic and confusion) Flow head sheets! Haul in spanker boom! Let go lee main braces, main tack and sheet! Clear away main bowlines! Clear away the lee lifeboat! Main clew garnets and buntlines! Up mainsail! Brace aback."

Would the *Jeanie Johnston*'s crew members be held to that same degree of knowledge and discipline? Would they work as hard as those seamen of another day, who were virtually captive slaves once they were aboard a ship and under the thumb of a ruthless captain? We would, after all, be sailors of a different stripe-- better educated, more sophisticated, conscious of our individual rights. And yet the sea, the weather and the potential dangers have not changed. How would the *Jeanie Johnston* handle this seeming dichotomy?

The Crew Book Captain Forwood had sent me put it in plain language: "If you are on the ship, you will be a member of the crew, and you will be expected to undertake every task on the ship-- set the sails, stow the sails, clean the ship daily, wash the deck, assist the Cook in the galley, maintain the ship under the guidance of the Bosun and steer the ship at all times, even in and out of port."

During the voyage, said the book, everyone on the ship, including the Captain, will stand watch. "You will be on duty for four hours at a time and have eight hours off duty. However, you will be expected to work at other times as the weather changes and sails need to be set or handed. All the crew without exception will have a long day."

I especially liked the Crew Book's introductory words, which presented either a threat or a challenge, depending on your mindset: "Before joining the *Jeanie Johnston* you may have formed some ideas of what a voyage on the ship will be like. You may have seen a video or attended a course of basic training. Whilst this will have been useful in preparing you for the voyage, the reality once the ship leaves the quayside will be quite different, and you may wonder exactly what you have let yourself in for.

"For instance, you will be living amongst strangers, trying to store a lot of information, and on top of all that you will be tired as a result of the work. What may appear to be confusion at the start will become clearer as time progresses, and you will find the work challenging as well as demanding. Gradually you will become focused on the immediate duties and the excitement of the days ahead and the ports and places you will visit. You may forget what day of the week it is and what is going on in the world back home. This will almost certainly be the case on the transatlantic voyage. It may well be that when the voyage comes to an end you may not want to go home."

Those words had almost certainly been written by Captain Mike Forwood himself. They reflected the language of a Cornish seafaring man and the vision of a consummate sailor who has experienced first hand how the sea can wrap its magic salty mantle around the hearts and souls of those who fall under its spell.

The Crew Book touched on many other areas of useful knowledge-- safety, health, the conditions of booking, code of conduct, and the ship's specifications. There were also some hints on "what to bring," and that touched off a new line of thought:

How do you pack for a 40-some day voyage across the Atlantic on a square-rigged ship?

My first thought was "With the wind whistling through the rigging and icy water sluicing across the deck, it's going to be cold." At a store catering to surfers, I found neoprene gloves, a neoprene shirt and neoprene boot liners. Then, to make sure, I went to outlets frequented by commercial fishermen. There I bought a heavy hooded jacket and rubberized gloves with textured palms to keep my hands dry and give me a grip when handling sheets and lines.

The *Jeanie Johnston* was scheduled to sail in May. I remembered the previous May when I sailed *Second Wind* from New Jersey to the Chesapeake. May can be a fresh wind blowing over 50-degree water, penetrating to your very bones.

Then there was the question of how much to bring. The crew book listed "sleeping bag, towels, trousers and shorts, sweaters, warm jacket, woolly hat, socks, shirts, plenty of underwear." Did "plenty of underwear" mean there won't be any chance to do laundry? I made a note to find out.

The ship would supply "waterproofs and seaboots." I decided I'd bring two pairs of boat shoes and my favorite light Gore-Tex jacket and sailing hat.

In addition to clothing and toilet articles, there are the neces-

44

sities of life-- laptop computer, two cameras, loads of film, batteries, notebooks, multi-band radio and miniature binoculars.

Should I take my GPS, or is it sacrilege to carry the tools of satellite navigation aboard a 19th Century ship? It would be fun to double-check the ship's daily position, and the GPS doesn't occupy much space. I decided to take it.

And then there were books. Ah, books. They're heavy, so there would be some difficult choices. I planned to take *The Art of Rigging*, a famous 19th Century book that tells you how to "reeve the gear and bend the royals," among other things; *Ship Fever*, a collection of stories; *Famine Ship Diary*, a personal account of an 1847 Atlantic crossing; a *Guide to Sea and Coastal Birds*; *Square Rigged Sailing Ships*, full of pictures, diagrams and sail plans; *1,000 Years of Irish Poetry,* a favorite; *The Wind in the Willows,* which I never finished reading; and at least two Patrick O'Brian novels. When O'Brian described tacking maneuvers and deck action during a sea battle, I'd be able to imagine it all taking place before my very eyes.

The Coast Guard Auxiliary alone was a treasure trove. I was especially fond of my old *Advanced Coastal Navigation* textbook, with its comprehensive scope and little human touches ("Stay humble; remember, it is arrogant to sail <u>to</u> a destination and appropriately humble to sail <u>towards</u> a destination."). But we'd see only two coasts -- the one we left behind and the one we were aiming for-- so "coastal" might not be too useful a category. I'd never studied celestial navigation, and the Crew Book said there would be ample opportunity on the transatlantic voyage to study and practice navigation, so maybe this would be my chance.

The AUXWEA (*Weather*) textbook might help me identify clouds, and it has pertinent chapters on pressure systems and tropical storms, including hurricanes. I figured I'd make copies of those chapters. The AUXOP *Seamanship* book probably would be the most useful reference of all; it touches on everything from knots and boat handling to NAVRULES and courtesy afloat.

Finally, there was the matter of jewelry. Yes, jewelry. The Crew Book said "The wearing of jewelry should be limited to close fitting items to the body that will not present a hazard to the wearer." Marie, a good Catholic, had bought me a fine medal of St. Christopher, patron saint of travelers; and then, for good measure, an even finer medal of St. Brendan the Navigator, patron of sailors, both to be worn on neck chains. I teased her about the double coverage, saying the last thing I wanted on the voyage was the distraction of having two saints fight for the right to save me should the occasion arise. In reality, I welcomed their presence. Life is full of mysteries, and who am I to doubt the intercession of saints? Besides, just knowing they were there might make me more aware of the need to avoid situations where their help would be required. And since they'd be under my shirt, I wouldn't be breaking the rule.

I was floating now on a cloud of tall ship hubris, and I wanted the whole world to feel as exuberant about the upcoming voyage as I did. Couldn't I get the Coast Guard Auxiliary into this act somehow, I wondered?

The Auxiliary is an organization of dedicated civilian volunteers who help the Coast Guard perform all their missions except law enforcement. They conduct on-water patrols, teach public education courses in boating safety, stand watch at Coast Guard Stations and join in search and rescue missions. I'd joined about the time I bought *Second Wind*, and I owed them a lot. At a time when I needed friends, I found them-- sea-loving, boat-loving friends and knowledgeable seamen all, and we'd had some memorable times together, sailing *Second Wind* down to the Chesapeake in the spring and back in the fall, and cruises full of fun and fellowship to Annapolis, St. Michaels, Solomons and Baltimore.

And then there were the training courses in seamanship, weather, navigation, search and rescue, some of them fairly challenging and all of them useful in focusing my attention and pulling my head together at a time when I badly needed it. It was the Auxiliary, more than any other factor, that had given me the heart to attempt the *Jeanie Johnston* crew quest. When I told my boating friends what I had in mind, they encouraged me at every step of the way. Yes, I owed the Auxiliary, and here was an opportunity for me to do something for them.

How about arranging for them to adopt the *Jeanie Johnston*, follow her voyage and greet her when she made port this side of the Atlantic? Now that the folks in Ireland had, against all odds, accepted me for a crew slot, anything seemed possible.

I tried the idea out on Bob Myers, then my Auxiliary Division Captain. "We could have the Auxiliary issue a kind of certificate of welcome to American waters," I suggested, "and I could present it to the Captain before the sailing." The occasion would make a good photo op, but more than that, it would show the Auxiliary at its best, emphasizing its concern for safety at sea and identifying itself with the openness of our society and the good will being lavished on the Irish/American community.

Bob thought the concept had merit, and we batted it back and forth, producing more ideas. I could provide a daily update by satellite link during the voyage, and we'd post it on the Auxiliary web site, helping to publicize the voyage throughout the Auxiliary system. If we could generate enough interest, we might get Auxiliarists to take to the water in their own boats, meet the ship and escort her into port, especially in Washington, her first and prime landfall.

"I think the best way to do this," said Bob, "is for me to pave the way with the National Commodore and put you in touch with him directly."

Meanwhile, I had written what I thought would be an appropriate certificate of welcome:

COMMEMORATING THE
JEANIE JOHNSTON MILLENNIUM VOYAGE
The United States Coast Guard Auxiliary

Salutes the Vision
Of the Jeanie Johnston's Builders
And the Courage and Commitment of Her Officers and Crew
We Wish You a Safe and Successful Voyage
And Extend a Hearty Welcome to American Waters
In the Spirit of an Old Irish Blessing
May Your Winds Be Fresh
Your Sails Full
And Your Wake Clean and Straight

Once Bob had made his contact, I emailed this, along with the ideas we had discussed, to the Commodore, and we talked briefly on the phone. Next day he was back to me via email. I'd receive the finished certificate, in plaque form, the following week. People would be calling me about public affairs support, and others would contact me about putting voyage reports on the AUXWEB. He'd like a letter from the *Jeanie Johnston* Project confirming the ideas of "Auxiliary sponsorship" while the ship is in the US, and asked me to get from her master the planned schedule of her US port visits, locations and dates. His final sentence was all I could have asked for: "Thanks to you for bringing this great opportunity to the Auxiliary."

Bob got carried away when I gave him that news. "Marie, he wrote in an email footnote, "please make sure Tom is not holding up a tankard of whatever it is the Irish are known to consume when they take his picture for the cover of *The Navigator*"(The Auxiliary's national publication).

Enthusiasm was building on the other side of the Atlantic too. "All of us at the *Jeanie Johnston* project are thrilled that the US Coast Guard Auxiliary has unofficially 'adopted' the *Jeanie Johnston* and is willing to help spread the word about the voyage and welcome the ship to American waters," John Griffin wrote to the National Commodore.

Emails began flowing from the Auxiliary webmaster and the national public affairs officers, and in no time at all notices were

48

appearing on various web pages: "USCG Auxiliary Sponsors Sailing Ship. . .The Auxiliary has 'adopted' the tall ship *Jeanie Johnston*. . .Auxiliarist Tom Kindre will provide daily updates for posting on this web site. . .A series of special Auxiliary events is being planned at each of the 23 ports on her itinerary (I hadn't even known about this). . .Steps are being taken to en-courage Auxiliary boats to meet the ship at each of her stops and escort her into port."

A new Auxiliary e-magazine, SITREP (Situation Report), was just being developed, and its creator, public affairs officer Fred Gates, in California, would soon become a regular email pen pal of mine. "We plan to publish accounts of you and the *Jeanie Johnston* regularly," Fred wrote."When the web page is up and running, your trip will be highlighted at the top of the page with a logo and a button readers can click on to jump straight to your story."

"Tom, this is very exciting," he went on. "This is some-thing new for the Auxiliary, reporting on a national event as it happens, and you and the *Jeanie Johnston* will add to the color and texture of the event for our members."

As I look back now on those heady exchanges, I wonder at what an innocent I was. The leprechauns were even then gather-ing their strength, lying in wait and preparing to attack, and I had no idea of the depth of their cunning or the amount of damage they could do. There had been clues, but I was too besotted with the glory of my undertaking to see them or to pay any attention if I did.

And all the while, the limb I was out on was getting longer and longer. "One of the men in our class is about to embark on the adventure of a lifetime," said the instructor in one of my Auxiliary courses. "Tom, tell us about your upcoming trip." No flotilla meeting went by without the flotilla commander ask-ing me to give an update on my forthcoming voyage, and my fellow Auxiliarists expressed suitable wonder and amazement.

The aura of heroic expectation was heightened immeasurably

when an article about the voyage and my part in it appeared in our regional daily newspaper, *The Asbury Park Press*. A staff writer had interviewed me aboard *Second Wind* while I was preparing her for her now-annual voyage to the Chesapeake, and his accompanying photographer had shot pictures of me fussing with the boat. I had told the writer some of my personal story about buying the boat, finding Marie, our discovery in Ireland of the embryonic ship struggling to be born in the little shipyard down the road in Blennerville, and about how the romantic notion of becoming a crew member had slowly grown on me. The story, a rather longish one with photos, appeared in the Easter Sunday edition, in a feature slot called *Turning Point-- Life's Challenges and Choices*.

Copies soon appeared on bulletin boards at the fitness center and the yacht club; and my alma mater, Rutgers University, where I was an active alumnus, ran stories in two alumni magazines. Now I was accosted by friends on all sides-- at the fitness center, at the Auxiliary, at Rutgers, at the yacht club. "How did you ever get into such an adventure?. . .When are you leaving?. . .What will you have to do as a crew member?. . .Is Marie going with you?. . .Are you sure you can get to the top of that mast when you have to?"

"We'll want you to give an illustrated lecture when you get back," said the yacht club commodore. The Brielle Seniors Club also wanted me as a speaker shortly after my return, and there was a call from the Women's Club with a similar request. They were all eager to put me on their calendars for an early September program, and I saw no reason why that wouldn't work, since we were sailing in May and arriving at the end of June or early July at the latest. That would surely give me adequate time to sort out photos and put some kind of presentation together.

The plaque arrived, rushed by express mail from Auxiliary headquarters, followed by a phone call from the Auxiliary officer who had expedited it. "I know you're leaving momentarily," he said, "and we wanted to be sure you received it in time." It was a handsome piece, with the Auxiliary logo in full color, mounted on a dark hardwood board. At the bottom was the commodore's signature, followed by the date: May 2000. It was of a good size and fairly heavy, so I put it in the bottom of my already-packed duffle bag, where it provided a firm foundation for everything else.

All the tenuously trailing threads seemed to be coming together now, and at that very moment one more event took place that appeared to telegraph the long-hoped-for moment when the *Jeanie Johnston* would finally up anchor, raise sail, turn her prow to the west and sail off into history. The word from Ireland was that the ship had been launched, its masts stepped, and it had had its official dedication and naming ceremonies.

"*Jeanie Johnston* Begins Voyage" said one of the Irish headlines. I knew that was a downright exaggeration; Captain Forwood had assured me that he would let me know far enough in advance to buy an airline ticket and arrive in Tralee in time for a week of crew training prior to the departure date. But it was indicative of the eagerness with which the media, the government and everyone else wanted the ship to fulfill her mission.

The launching was not without its complications. The original plan had been to launch the ship directly from the shipyard of her birth at Blennerville, but while a channel was being dredged, the remains of a 19th century ship were discovered. Archeology won out over engineering, and the planners had to find a new plan. They towed a huge shallow-draft barge from the Netherlands, laboriously moved the ship onto it via a 72-wheel platform, then floated the barge and towed it to Fenit, the nearest deep-water port on the Bay of Tralee. The barge was then submerged, and the *Jeanie Johnston* floated free for the first time.

The complex procedure drew huge crowds, and the celebrations were typically Irish. The day the ship was moved aboard the barge was to have been the official launching day, but bad weather and an ebbing tide prevented the barge from moving out and forced a delay. The visitors, though, were in no mood to put off their festivities. "Sandwiches had been made," said the local newspaper, "and there was plenty of beer, so, being who we are, we decided to have a party anyhow."

Later, the three-mile voyage to Fenit aboard the barge turned into a stately progress as thousands of cheering onlookers lined the shoreline and a local piper played a lament as the barge passed the old famine emigrant quay at Blennerville.

There were dignitaries and speeches aplenty at the launching and ensuing dedication, but the most touching words may have been those of Alice, who answered the phone in Captain Forwood's office when I called. "I've been here since the beginning," she said, "and the ship is like my very own baby." How did the ship react when she was launched? "They said if she were to groan when she was lifted," said Alice, "it would mean she's not watertight, but she went in without a whisper, and we all cheered."

Then, in what looked for all the world like a finishing touch, the *Jeanie Johnston*'s blond-haired figurehead, carved by a noted Irish sculptor and painted in Kerry green and gold, was fitted to her prow.

All this I learned informally from telephone calls to the Project, information on web sites in Kerry and Irish newspapers accessed over the Internet. All I knew officially was that Captain Forwood would call me when it was time to report for duty.

A small worm gnawed at the edge of my emotional high. The complications of the launching must have taken more time than anyone expected. Would this mean more delay? And why was there no longer an official sailing date, just "late in May?" But I put those negative thoughts aside and basked in my own vision of the upcoming voyage.

I was packed and ready. All I needed was the word to go.

Above (L): Great slabs of Irish oak, gleaned mostly from trees felled by a storm, are cut into beam size and kept moist. *Above (R):* Rough beams are prepared for forming into frames. *(Below):* The men who proudly built the Jeanie Johnston.

Above: Giant frames are added to the keel, one after another, until the full length of the ship is defined. *Below:* Ensuring that the ship's skeleton is trim and straight. There is plenty of close work in tight spaces for patient woodworkers.

Above (L): Young carpenters and apprentices from several countries converged on the Blennerville shipyard to help. *Above (R):* The hull shape can be seen as frames are assembled. *Below:* Deck layout is prepared before deck is planked.

Above: The ship's hull, now fully planked, is placed under a protective canopy, where work can continue in all weather. *Below (L):* A carpenter's apprentice at work in the shipyard. *Below (R):* Engineer Peter O'Regan checks an alignment.

Above: With the hull completed, the ship is moved to a huge barge, which transports it to nearby Fenit. The rainbow is surely a good omen *Below:* Smiles of appreciation when the engines and generators have been successfully installed.

Above (L): Masts in the Blennerville yard awaiting their installation. *Above (R):* Masts are stepped while the ship is on the barge. *Below:* On a foggy day, the Jeanie Johnston sits in its Fenit berth during the final months of its fitting-out.

CHAPTER 5
Slipping Away Into the Future

Cracks had begun to appear in the *Jeanie Johnston* millennial voyage plan even as I pursued my frantic campaign to gain a crew berth, but, ostrich-like, I had consistently ignored them. Now they were widening and deepening as the weeks passed.

An early brochure had listed 29 ports in the US, Canada and Ireland to be visited by the ship between May 15, 2000 and January 27 of the following year. The first-- and the ship's North American landfall-- was Washington, DC, where President Clinton, on a visit to the *Jeanie Johnston* site in Tralee, had promised to come aboard and greet the Captain and crew. For 10 days surrounding the Fourth of July weekend, the ship was to be at New York City's South Street Seaport, playing a major role in the city's Op Sail celebration.

At the bottom of the port itinerary page a note, in small type, warned that this was a "draft timetable; may be slight alterations." That proved to be a considerable understatement.

The original sailing date from Ireland was listed as April 15. At the time I was negotiating for a crew berth, it had slipped to May 7; and by the time I was accepted, it stood at "sometime in May." By the end of April, I was told that the earliest possible sailing date was the end of May, and there was a "big question mark" next to that. Captain Forwood wrote a day or two later,

"At this moment, there is no firm sailing date, but naturally as soon as we can, we will let you know the date so you can make your arrangements to travel here to join the ship."

Meanwhile, National Commodore Tucker of the Coast Guard Auxiliary was pressuring me for firm dates and locations of US port visits so he could send directives to all pertinent Auxiliary districts to involve them in activities aimed at welcoming the ship to American waters.

The next few weeks were a time of utter frustration. I was simultaneously gathering information on airline flights, trying to determine when I should book one and pressing for details of the ship's schedule and port itinerary for the Auxiliary. The people in Ireland had become increasingly cautious in their statements, and there were no longer any port lists or firm dates for the maiden voyage or the port visits.

Finally, in mid-May, I was informed unofficially by Captain Forwood's office that the ship would not sail before June 15. That meant that the OpSail plans for the *Jeanie Johnston* were totally out of the window, since there was no way she could cross the Atlantic and be on the US East Coast by the Fourth of July. Her participation in the celebrations in New York, Boston and elsewhere was to have been the centerpiece of her visit, the jubilant conclusion of her maiden voyage. She was to have paraded triumphantly through New York Harbor as the newest and most noteworthy tall ship on the block. Now she would be notable for her absence.

"Tall ship fever has engulfed the US East Coast," I wrote on the Auxiliary web page, "with OpSail 2000 and TallShips 2000 fleets converging into an array of races, port visits, parades and special events. But one tall ship will not be among them. The *Jeanie Johnston*, the replica 19th century emigrant ship, will not sail in time to participate in the New York, Boston and Chicago tall ship events."

How could I convey the disappointing news to the National Commodore? He had pulled all the stops to get that plaque ready in time for me to fly to Ireland and present it to the *Jeanie Johnston*'s master on that glorious day in May when she was to up anchor and set sail. He had alerted his public affairs officers to coordinate plans to celebrate the ship's arrival in each US port she would visit and find ways to motivate Auxiliarists to sail their own boats out to greet her.

All I could do was grit my teeth and send him a letter of explanation and apology. It wasn't easy.

I tried hard to look on the bright side of this news, if there was one. Long after the parties and the fireworks, I speculated, a lone ship would make her way across the Atlantic, having the spotlight all to herself. Her arrival would be the culminating tall ship event of the Millennial Year.

But not everyone was buying my reinterpretation of the voyage delay. "Are you sure there's actually a ship over there?" was a typical question. "Do those people know what they're doing?" or "Do you think the Irish can get their act together and pull this off, or are they really out of their depth?"

Greetings from friends I hadn't seen in a few weeks followed a progressive pattern over time. At first, it was, "Oh, I see you haven't gone yet," then, "Oh, you're still here!" And finally, "You must be back from your sailing trip. How was it?"

By this time, various alternative options were being discussed in Tralee, and the information I could extract depended on how close a relationship I had with the person I was talking to. One confidante had told me, when the OpSail linkup seemed still a possibility, that the ship would most likely skip Washington and head straight for New York, then make its way up the coast to Boston.

A few weeks later I was told unofficially that the sailing date had slipped to the end of June. And in early June, after I had complained vigorously to the Project management in Tralee that we were letting the Auxiliary down, I received the news that it would take another month to complete the ship and conduct her sea trials. The expectation was that she would sail at the end of

July or early August and make landfall by early September in Quebec, where the original Jeanie Johnston had been built. From there she would head south for a rendezvous with President Clinton in Washington, complete a tour of major East Coast cities in October and November, winter over in Florida and visit the Great Lakes ports in 2001.

First the destination port had been Washington. Then New York. Now it was Quebec. Originally, Marie was to have met me in Washington at the conclusion of the voyage. Then the plan was changed to a meeting in New York, simpler and closer to home. Now she would have to journey to Quebec, which was considerably farther away. Travel plans were discussed, tentatively agreed upon and then discarded, one after another.

Our plans for the tall ship festival in New York had gone through a similar evolution. When the ship was scheduled to make landfall in Washington, our voyage crew would have departed there, but we would have delighted later in seeing the *Jeanie Johnston* at the tall ship parade in New York. Then, when her arrival port was changed to New York, I had the heady prospect of being aboard myself when she paraded up New York Harbor and the Hudson River. Now we'd have to see Op-Sail without the *Jeanie Johnston*. That would take some luster off the experience, but on the other hand it could be an exciting prelude to the voyage, now likely (I no longer used the word "scheduled") to take place about a month later.

While these thoughts were still in our minds, an invitation arrived from Ireland. It was on a gold-bordered card, and it required an RSVP. Commodore J.J. Kavanagh, Flag Officer Commanding the Irish Naval Service, and Commander James Robinson, DSM, Commanding Officer of the Irish Naval Flagship *L.E. Eithne,* in salute to the *Jeanie Johnston* Tall Ship Project, were requesting the pleasure of my company at a reception aboard the *L,E. Eithne* at Pier 90, West 50th Street, New York on July 5th.

An opportunity to see and board the flagship of the Irish

Navy doesn't come along every day, and I thought I'd better take advantage of it. The summons sounded formal, but then these things always do. Uniform or business attire was permitted, so attendees would be a mixed lot, and I looked forward to meeting some of the project staff from Tralee as well as members of the Irish/American community who were backing the voyage. They might have an inside track on the latest information, and I had questions that needed answers.

Marie and I presented the gold-edged invitation at Pier 90 on July 5 and were ushered to the gangplank and thence aboard the *Eithne*. She was not a large ship, but her neighbor at the next pier was so formidable that she appeared smaller than she was. There, sitting a few yards across the water, was the US aircraft carrier *Kennedy*, in town for the OpSail celebration. She was so huge, so tall, so overpowering, that we felt like Lilliputians on a lilypad. We had seen the *Kennedy* the day before, during the tall ship parade, but not this close up. An uneasiness hung over us, as though we were under scrutiny from Big Brother, but we soon managed to forget the surroundings and fall into the spirit of the occasion. The Guinness was flowing, and the talk and the laughter were so boisterous they must have kept the off-duty sailors on the *Kennedy* awake, even through that great steel hull.

John Griffin, the *Jeanie Johnston* project manager, emerged from the crowd and we chatted briefly, almost shouting to be heard. New competition soon arose when the singing stars from *Riverdance*, then on Broadway, began their performance. Amid the melee, I found Ann Martin, the Project's marketing executive, with whom I had first corresponded, and we exchanged a few words, but most of what I wanted to hear was drowned out. Commander Robinson, the ship's commanding officer, introduced himself, and, walking away from the center of activity, we talked about the Irish Navy, of which I had known nothing until that very moment.

The Navy, which consists of eight ships, had its beginning after World War II when Ireland acquired a handful of corvettes--

those tough, stubby little vessels that had shepherded Atlantic convoys and hunted Nazi U-boats, dropping depth charges off their afterdecks. In time the corvettes evolved into increasingly sophisticated offshore patrol ships, some of which took on specialized duties. The *Eithne* was built as a long-range fisheries patrol ship, intended to be at sea for up to 19 days. She is the first Irish ship to carry a helicopter, and the broad, flat afterdeck on which all the shouting, singing and stomping was taking place was her helicopter landing pad.

Home port for the Navy is Haulbowline, near the Irish south coast port of Cobh. The name evokes the age of square-rigged ships, but the flotilla's duties are strictly related to today's challenges-- running drug interdiction missions, attempting to thwart clandestine migration and protecting fishery operations-- much the same as those of the US Coast Guard.

"I can't give you a tour of the ship's inner spaces because of security," said Commander Robinson, "but if you step up to the forward end of this deck you'll see a diagram of all the decks and get an idea of what's located where."

As the evening wore on, the din increased. The Guinness flowed more freely and the tempo of the music stepped up, with singing and step dancing now competing with the burgeoning flood of voices. The sound waves spiraled up into the soft Hudson River night, and I was convinced that even an observer on another planet would have been aware of this small pulsating square of sound, light and activity.

The Irish have a name for this phenomenon. They call it "the craic," pronounced "crack." A knowledgeable Irish friend defines the word as "an enjoyable social situation with friends or family, usually accompanied by alcohol consumption and spiced with humor." A typical conversation after such an event might go as follows: "Well, did you enjoy yourselves, then?" Answer: "Sure, the craic was mighty!"

Moving off to the edge of the craic, we met an official of the Ancient Order of Hibernians, who are ardent supporters of the

Jeanie Johnston project. He, in turn, introduced us to a young apprentice carpenter from Trenton, New Jersey, who had spent three months earlier in the year as a volunteer worker, sponsored by the carpenters' union, fastening Austrian larch planking to the Irish oak frames of the *Jeanie Johnston*. "It was a fascinating experience," he said. In Ireland he had met the girl who would become his wife, and they were married in two ceremonies, one in Ireland and one in New Jersey. "Another apprentice," said the Hibernian official, "was so impressed by the ship he plans to be married aboard it when the *Jeanie Johnston* comes to the US."

"What a shame," he went on, "that the ship won't be making its maiden voyage until next spring."

"That's not so," I said. "I'm going to be on the crew. I know the ship will be sailing this year-- probably about the end of July or early August."

He looked at me blankly but said nothing.

Finally we decided to follow Commander Robinson's suggestion, walked to the forward end of the deck and studied the diagram of the *Eithne*'s interior displayed there on an easel. Next to the easel I noticed a large open carton filled with what looked like press kits. Press kits are not meant to blush unseen, so I helped myself to one. Putting aside the background pieces, I plucked out the principal release and began to read:

"Irish Naval Flagship L.E. Eithne Salutes
The Jeanie Johnston Project in New York on July 5

On July 5th, Commodore J.J. Kavanagh and Commander James Robinson DSM, of the Irish Navy, will host a reception for the Jeanie Johnston Project on board the Irish Naval Flagship L.E. Eithne. Brian Kennedy and Sara Clancy, singing stars of Riverdance on Broadway, will perform in honor of the Jeanie Johnston.

L.E. Eithne is visiting New York to participate in the International Naval Review 2000, a symbol of the international good will of the United States of America, in which naval vessels from 24 nations take part. The review, held in conjunction with Military Salute Week and New York City's July 4th Millennium celebration, will be the largest celebration event in US history.
The Jeanie Johnston-- the replica Irish 19th century emigrant ship-- which is currently nearing completion at Fenit, County Kerry, will make a farewell tour of Ireland prior to its planned North American voyage. The ship is now due for completion in August and following sea trials will undertake a tour of the major Irish ports, North and South, including Limerick, Galway, Derry, Belfast, Dublin, Waterford and Cork. This will afford the general public and project supporters throughout Ireland the opportunity to visit the ship before she sets sail to America early in 2001."

Wait a minute. What was going on here? This had to be a mistake. The ship was sailing in 2001? That was next year! No one had told me about this. I began to feel my blood pressure rising but continued to read, as though hoping to learn that this was a joke that would be explained away in the next paragraph:

"The company had considered sailing the ship to America later this year and wintering her on the East Coast but decided against this because of weather and in an effort to attend popular North American Irish festivals beginning early next year. The ship is now due in North America in the Spring of 2001 and will visit over 20 US and Canadian cities over a 9-month period."

The look on the Hibernian official's face came back to me. He'd known something I didn't know, and this obviously was it. Thoughts raced through my head. What was this about the weather? Well, they had a point there. We were already well into the hurricane season, and if the ship didn't sail until August, we could be courting hurricanes before the end of the voyage. There was no certain way to know about hurricanes in advance, and the safest course was to complete a transatlantic voyage by June, which was generally agreed to be the start of the Atlantic hurricane season, or shortly afterward. It was already July, so that insurance plan was no longer available.

As for the "popular North American Irish festivals," they surely meant St. Patrick's Day, but that would require a voyage well in advance of spring, and the release said the ship was now due in North America in the spring of 2001. But of all the questions raised by this announcement, the most troubling were (1) Why was the news of postponement buried in what purported to be a news release about the *Eithne*'s New York port visit? and (2) Why hadn't I, as a crew member, been notified?

While Marie sought refuge in a quiet corner, I fought my way back through the crowd and found John Griffin. "John, I've just seen this press release for the first time. Why weren't crew members notified of this? People are rearranging their lives to be part of this venture, and then they're totally ignored when changes are made. That's not right!"

I was wound up. John Griffin let me unwind a bit, then he said "Yes, our communications are at fault. Captain Forwood was away when this decision was made, and it's his responsibility to be in touch with crew members, so unfortunately there was a vacuum. You see, the *Eithne* event was organized long before this postponement was considered, but it brought the matter to a head. I made the official announcement here in New York yesterday. I'm sorry you weren't informed."

I was slightly mollified but would still have left in a huff if he hadn't added "Meanwhile, we'd like to invite you to be our guest on the ship for at least part of the round-Ireland tour."

What a splendid idea! This man knew his way to my heart,

61

and I felt my angry feelings slowly dissolving. Sailing around Ireland would be a great opportunity to get to know the ship under more benign circumstances than in the middle of the Atlantic, and more important, to get to know and work with the crew.

Over the next couple of days, I tried to sort out the real reasons behind the delay. Were the leprechauns out to wreck this grand project? I knew they were mischievous creatures, but didn't they have a sense of national pride?

Maybe it wasn't the leprechauns at all, but Murphy who was doing it. My *Book of Irish Blessings and Sayings* includes Murphy's Law, which, as we all know, says "Nothing is as easy as it looks. Everything takes longer than you expect. And if anything can go wrong, it will."

Surely, the leprechauns and Murphy together could be a formidable combination, though the *Jeanie Johnston* Project office, to their credit, refrained from hiding behind such obvious excuses. John Griffin was quoted on the County Kerry web page as saying that one of the great challenges of the project was its dual nature-- building a faithful historic replica while at the same time complying with modern maritime regulations. That, plus bad weather at the work site, was why the fitting out was proving so time-consuming. It was also proving costly. A IR£2 million cost overrun required action by the Irish government, but the funding was secured and the work would continue.

I called Captain Forwood to try to pin down the timing of the "spring" voyage and found myself in for another shock.

"We'll be leaving on January 7," he said, and I immediately had visions of frozen hands grasping ice-covered shrouds and ratlines. But I recovered slightly as he talked. We'd be heading south as fast as the wind could take us, he told me. What's more, January in Ireland averages between 41 and 45 degrees Fahrenheit, courtesy of the Gulf Stream. That news eased the chill a bit, but still, why were we leaving in the middle of winter?

It seems that the Project's directors, along with their many Irish/American friends and support groups, had decided it would be symbolically important to make landfall in the US by St. Patrick's Day. To the Irish, St. Partick's Day is spring. No matter that our voyage would take place in the winter; it would be a spring voyage.

The plan was to weigh anchor on January 7 and sail the southern route, via Lisbon, the Canaries, Puerto Rico and Fort Lauderdale, arriving in Savannah on March 14. That's a voyage of some 5,000 miles, with an overall elapsed time of some 67 days. Part of that time would be spent in ports along the way.

"Wind and weather permitting," said the Captain, "we'll spend a couple of days in each port. Depending on what we encounter, we might pop into a port we weren't expecting to see. If we're chased by a northwest gale, for example, we might flip into La Coruna, on the Spanish coast. If the weather is good, we'll have more leeway for port stays."

From a web site devoted to international weather, I printed out an interesting color diagram entitled "Storm Tracks Over the North Atlantic and Europe." It showed that over a period of 10 Januarys, four storms crossed our projected route. Statistically, at least, we had a 60 percent chance of choosing a year with no storms. But who knows? The statistical data might include four one-storm years, or it might be based on one four-storm year and nine years with none. We can only wait and see.

In the Canaries, the Captain said, we'd make port in either Tenerife or La Palma. Just the name, "The Canaries," evokes the romance of voyages. In the 16th century, the islands became a major supply base for ships bound for the Spanish colonies in the West Indies and South America, and they were attacked from time to time by such great English captains as Drake, Hawkins, Blake and Nelson.

Even centuries before that, they had navigational significance. Ferro, the most westerly of the islands, was also the most westerly known place in the ancient world, and in A.D. 150 Ptolemy chose it for the prime meridian of longitude. Even into the late 18th century, some navigators still reckoned their distances from this line before Greenwich was finally established as the internationally approved site. I was looking forward to the Canaries. There would be a lot of history to ponder when I'm there.

Our sea route was a logical one, if we were looking for the best benefits of prevailing currents and winds, and for that reason we would be following in the wake of many others who went this way before us.

The navigator who pioneered our projected route was the Admiral of the Ocean Sea himself, Christopher Columbus. His first voyage, from Palos, Spain in 1492, followed a track slightly to the north of ours. The route of his second voyage, which left from Cadiz the following year, is close to the one we were to follow. We can assume that what he learned from the first voyage was incorporated into his planning for the second. In each case, he stopped at the Canaries and picked up the southern trade winds to carry him west. On voyage No. 2, he made landfall near Dominica in the Lesser Antilles and then passed close to Puerto Rico on his way to Hispaniola. More than 500 years later, we would come close to duplicating that track.

When we did-- if we did-- it would be a good six months away, and into the next year to boot. Some friends were now beginning to doubt the voyage would ever take place; others were telling me it didn't make any sense and I ought simply to forget about it.

"Why, at your age," some asked, "are you going to make that long, difficult trip on a wooden ship, subject to God knows what kind of weather, working hard all day, knocking yourself out when you could be at home relaxing the way a retired person should?" The reporter who interviewed me for the newspaper story put it even more pointedly: "Why risk your nearly 80-year-old life and limb, climbing up and down towering masts, facing the turbulent seas day in and day out?"

So many people had asked such questions that I began to wonder myself. With all the delays, I now had plenty of time to think about it, and I reached some conclusions.

At first, I had simply said I considered it the adventure of a lifetime, and that's true. I couldn't conceive of anyone with an interest in sailing having the opportunity and the time to take a voyage like this one and not doing it.

When questioned further, I came up with a second reason: I would be forging a link with my past. My grandmother, Joanna O'Brien, born in County Cork, had boarded a ship like the *Jeanie Johnston* in Cobh when she was 16 and sailed for America. I'd be following in her footsteps, and I'd try to imagine how an uneducated Irish teenager might have reacted to the rigors of an ocean voyage. That's true, too. But there was more to it than that, and it came to me while I was listening to a CD of movie music.

I was an impressionable 14-year-old when the movie *Captain Blood* was released-- the first Hollywood film to star the exciting, swashbuckling young Errol Flynn. It had everything: stirring sea battles between square-rigged ships, breathtaking tacking duels, escaped slaves making off with a Spanish ship, a sword fight to the death with the villainous Basil Rathbone and a love interest in the beautiful Olivia DeHavilland, who immediately became my pin-up girl.

It also had a score by Viennese composer Erich Wolfgang Korngold that ushered in the great era of romantic movie music. Every note of it went straight into my memory cells, where it was to remain for the rest of my life.

Even now, I could hum or whistle the ship's theme, the love theme or the march of the Spanish soldiers. The ship's theme, on English and French horns, always rose to its blood-stirring crescendo when the sails were full and the ship had a bone in her teeth, with the bow wave hissing back on either side.

I wasn't raised in a boating family and was never on a sailboat until I was in my 40s, but sailing had become a great love of my life, and I think Flynn and Korngold had something to do with it. Their spell was there, buried, and it came out, as many youthful impressions do, later in life, when there's time to reflect on who we really are.

Once, aboard *Second Wind*, I had caught a glimpse of the connection.

We were running offshore from Atlantic City to Cape May, under jib and mizzen, with a 30-knot wind at our backs. There were 12-foot seas, and we were doing two knots above hull speed as we planed down the faces of the waves. The experience was so exhilarating that I was virtually beside myself, but I remembered later that from time to time I had been humming snatches of the *Captain Blood* score.

Why would I not miss the *Jeanie Johnston* voyage for anything? Because every time I picture the ship slicing cleanly through the waves with all her sails billowing out majestically, I hear Korngold's horns.

But dreams are fragile things. Unless they can continue-- if only by the thinnest of threads-- to offer their promise of eventual fulfillment, they are apt to wither and die. The *Jeanie Johnston* dream was still alive, but time was running out.

I remembered a line from the *Asbury Park Press* story that I had considered at the time to be somewhat florid language: "The vast expanse of the Atlantic Ocean," the reporter had written, "still calls out to him in the twilight of his life."

It was the first time anyone had placed me in that particular time frame. He was right, though. I had to accept the fact that I was in the twilight. I certainly wouldn't have another 20, 15 or even 10 years. Five? Who knows? I felt good and had no major ailments. Mentally and emotionally, I was much the same as I'd been at 20, though I felt better about a lot of things now, including myself, than I had then. Other than creaking bones, and less stamina than I once had, I was in good shape physically.

But daylight was fading, and I had many nautical miles to go before nightfall. Most important, I wanted to finish writing this book. But its *piece de resistance* would be the voyage itself-- without that there would be no book-- and the voyage kept slipping away into that misty, uncertain realm called The Future.

66

CHAPTER 6
The Great Lady Herself

At first, the round-Ireland tour planned for the fall of 2000 had all the earmarks of a grand triumphal progress. Limerick, Galway, Derry, Belfast, Dublin, Waterford and Cork were on the itinerary, and Dingle, Killebay and Londonderry were being considered. "Invitations to visit," said John Griffin, "are flying in." Mike Forwood hoped the ship would be ready by early October "because we have a planned program for Ireland starting October 15 and finishing in Dublin for the New Year. All transatlantic crew members can participate without cost in all or part of this voyage." There would be open house visits and parties for the crew at every stop.

That was at the beginning of August. By mid-month Mike had starkly different news: "I do not believe the ship will be ready until November and then will just visit Belfast and Dublin in December. The round-Ireland adventure was dwindling away and the possibility of it happening at all now seemed questionable.

The *Jeanie Johnston* might not be ready to sail, but I was more ready than I would ever be. I fretted with impatience and started avoiding friends who wondered why I wasn't at sea. What steps could I take to bridge this period of inactivity and renew my faith that the ship and the voyage were real? One thing I could do was go to Ireland and visit her.

Two circumstances now came together that offered just such an opportunity. First, Marie and I were to be on a college alumni tour of Provence in October, and we proposed to conclude that trip with a stay of several days in Paris. At that point, I would be in Europe, in no hurry to get home, so it would make sense to tack a few more days onto the itinerary and fly to Ireland.

The second factor was the discussions I had been having with the ship's project management about writing and producing a series of newsletters for dissemination in the US. The support of Irish/American communities in America was critical to the success of the project, and especially now that delay and uncertainty were in the air, there was a need to keep these crucial audiences informed. I volunteered my time and effort to write and edit the newsletters. I would be gathering material about the *Jeanie Johnston*'s construction and operating systems and at the same time getting to know some members of the permanent crew.

And so it was that I found myself in the Paris/DeGaulle Airport saying *au revoir* to Marie, who would fly home alone, and, with reduced luggage, setting out for a week in Tralee.

Flying into Shannon Airport from Europe, you cross all of Ireland before you land. That fabulous green mosaic, as you pass over it at low altitude, reveals at once the color and the tragic history of the nation. The color is bred of mists, vapors and weeping rainfalls, but the pattern of the green, divided as it is into infinitesimal squares, chunks, slices and shards, is a stark reminder of the process that subdivided Ireland into parcels of land so small that many were barely capable of sustaining a family on a crop of potatoes. The end result, when the potato famine struck, was a national disaster.

This route-- from Paris to Shannon-- is notable for another reason, too. It is, in reverse, the last leg of the historic solo flight of Charles Lindbergh. Lindbergh, swooping low over the west

coast of Ireland, had hailed fishermen to ask his way, crossed the green mosaic carpet and the Irish Sea, then flew over Southwest England and the English Channel before raising the delta of the Seine and flying into Paris and the history books.

Those thoughts were still in my head as I checked into my Tralee bed-and-breakfast, but they were quickly dispelled by the raucous entrance of a half dozen football players, still in uniform, who filled the lobby with their noise and their muscles. I had arrived, apparently, on a football weekend, with a championship at stake for the local Kerry team.

As soon as I could, I called a taxi and headed for the pier at Fenit. The *Jeanie Johnston* offices were closed until Monday, and though the rain was falling in rolling sheets, it was still daylight, so I might at least see the ship.

The pier office was closed too, but there the ship stood in her berth, defiant of the weather, her bowsprit jauntily cocked up at an acute angle, her rigging darkened by the rain and her spars glistening with the wet.

Her hull was complete, of course, and her deckhouses were semi-finished, so it was easy to get an overall picture of what she would look like when she headed into her historic voyage. Her lines are not sleek, like those of a clipper, but she is, after all, a square rigger, and her beauty is the kind that arises from a perfect marriage of form and function. "Sturdy" and "grand" are perhaps the best words to describe her.

Fenit, the deep water port for Tralee since the approach to Blennerville, its old port, had shoaled up, was simply a village with a long breakwater and dock protruding into the waters of Tralee Bay. The only other inhabitants of the dock were work boats and barges, and it was not hard to think of the *Jeanie Johnston* as a misplaced queen surrounded by lowly servants.

I had seen the ship at last; now I wanted to relax and savor that vision. My choices for dinner -- not wanting to walk too far in the rain-- were between a rowdy pub curiously named the Abbey House and a candlelit restaurant across the street called

The Cookery. I judiciously chose to have a pint of Guinness at the pub, where the loud talk was of nothing but football, and dinner at the Cookery, where a coal fire burned in the stove and the tall, slim waitresses were all in black, contributing to the illusion that it might have been a nunnery.

During the night, the streets echoed with the drunken shouts of football fans, and some time in the wee hours I heard loud knocking and heartfelt pleas in the hallway. The pleas had gone unanswered, apparently. When I emerged in the morning, a great hulk of a man, dressed in shorts, lay in the middle of the hall floor, snoring vigorously. I stepped over him carefully and made my way to the inn's full cooked Irish breakfast.

It was still raining, though with less energy, and I decided to walk the two miles or so to Blennerville, where two years earlier I had seen the first frames of the ship.

The place was deserted, and the visitor center, which I had missed seeing on that earlier trip, was locked. On a hunch, however, I went to the back, found an open door and took a self-conducted tour of the unlighted museum.

The informative exhibits illustrated the history of sailing ships, the potato famine, the famine ships and the genesis and goals of the *Jeanie Johnston* Project. The centerpiece was a scale model of the ship, about six feet long, which I studied for some time from a variety of angles.

As I stood there alone in the dim light, I felt I had made an important connection, and the rightness of my part in the forthcoming adventure struck me as it never had before.

My first visit the next day was with John Griffin, the project director. John was jaunty, friendly and voluble, though his Kerry dialect was sometimes a bit hard to follow. It was he who had had the initial vision of the *Jeanie Johnston*; but like all visionaries, he had soon learned that hard-edged realities could be daunting.

John, who had already rebuilt an historic railroad and windmill in County Kerry (the one I'd seen in Blennerville), dreamed

70

of building a replica of a famine-era Irish ship. But first a ship-yard had to be built, then a master shipwright found. His ad in the *Irish Skipper* caught the eye of Michael O'Boyle, who had built wooden ships all his working life but thought no one wanted them any more.

"I wonder do these people know what they're getting into," O'Boyle said he thought at the time, but "I had a sixth sense I'd get involved." His first job was to find 150-year-old oak trees to produce the huge frames. "There wasn't a forest in the country I didn't walk," he said. Larch for the planking had to be imported. Then the crying need was for shipwrights. "I'm trawling the world for men," said O'Boyle. He found some shipwrights and trained others. And then the O'Regan brothers came to the project.

Ciaran O'Regan and his brother Peter were masterminding the ship's construction. Ciaran, who had spent years building wooden vessels, was shipwright foreman. "This is going to resurrect the art of boat building in this area" is the way he saw it. Peter, as project engineer, had almost single-handedly de-signed and built all the ship's engineering systems. "He's a meticulous engineer," I was told, "and there's not a nut or a bolt aboard he doesn't know intimately."

From the moment John Griffin introduced me to Captain Mike Forwood, I felt positive emanations. Mike had been hired the previous September, and it seemed that the project could not have found a man better suited to the job.

For one thing, he fulfilled all my expectations of what a sea captain should look like. He was tall, rangy, weather-beaten and authoritatively bearded. But more than that, he had deep knowl-edge and command presence, a good combination of virtues for a man with his responsibilities. He proved to be friendly enough, but you always knew he was in charge. And as I got to know him over the next few days, he turned out to be a man whose vision cuts through rambling talk and fuzzy thinking and gets at once to the nub of what needs to be done and how it's to be accomplished. It was comforting to know the ship would be in his hands.

Mike hails from Cornwall. He went to sea as a teenager and had been sailing ever since. He had come to the *Jeanie Johnston* from his post as Senior Master and Marine Superintendent of the British Sail Training Association . As head of BSTA, he operated the three-masted schooners *Sir Winston Churchill* and *Malcolm Miller* and organized the international tall ship races. Before that, he sailed the Pacific as a master with P&O Lines. Back home in Cornwall, he told me, he sailed a Morecombe Bay Prawner, a 33-foot gaff-rigged cutter.

With the Captain as my guide, I had a tour of the ship, and I was impressed with the vessel's solidity. Her planking is four to five inches thick, and her frames are like tree trunks, which indeed they were cut from. And while she looks like a 19th century ship, she hardly is, with her five steel-bulkheaded watertight compartments, 280 hp diesels, 105 KVA generators, CO_2 system, multiphase electrical system, deep freeze unit, air conditioning and 4,000-liter-per-day water maker. Although the general outlines of the below-decks spaces were clearly visible, I was astonished at the amount of work that remained to be done. Dozens of workmen-- carpenters, electricians, fitters and riggers-- were clambering about, all pursuing their individual specialties.

We sat at a table in the Captain's office, and in an interview that lasted an hour or more, I extracted information from him on the ship's propulsion, communications, waste, drinking water and electrical systems, plus crew training, navigation, weather, safety and a few other subjects.

"Tom, I'm off to do some deck chores," said the Captain finally. "Want to join me?"

The sudden shift caught me by surprise, but remembering that I am also a signed-on crew member for the transatlantic voyage, I quickly said "Of course!"

Moments later, in a dock work shed, he thrust a brush into my hand and said, "Why don't you varnish those belaying pins?

72

I'll be back shortly," and off he went for some supplies.

Some 40 belaying pins later (I thought he might be testing me so I'd moved along smartly), he returned. "OK, now grab one of those safety belts off the wall hook. We're going out on the bowsprit." We clambered aboard the ship and made our way forward.

The bowsprit is in two sections, the larger of which is as big around as a medium-size tree, and it tilts slightly upward, extending 26 feet beyond the prow.

To get on it, you have to climb over the gunwale, which is some four feet high at that point, and no one has provided any steps or handholds to ease your way. You haul yourself up, straddle the gunwale, then put your feet over on the foot rope, which runs the length of the bowsprit about three feet below it, and clip your tether to a steel cable.

Your only other point of reference is the main chain, which runs back from the end of the bowsprit a few feet outboard of the foot rope. The angle narrows as you go forward, and, depending on where you're working, you can sit on the chain with your feet on the rope or you can walk or stand clumsily with one foot on the rope and the other on the chain. Below you is a three-inch mesh nylon net designed to catch you before you hit the water should anything break.

Our immediate job was to weave the loose strands at the edge of the net into a bolt rope, then lash the edge of the net to the bolt rope and finally, lash the bolt rope to the chain. The bolt rope wasn't long enough. The Captain handed me another length of rope and said "Tom, make a short splice, will you?" I hadn't made a splice for 20 or more years, and I'd forgotten the fine points if, indeed, I ever knew them. "Sorry," I said.

At that point, Sean, one of the teen-age trainees from Northern Ireland who had joined us, tried his hand at the job but was no more successful than I would have been. Captain Mike had to do it himself, and he showed us both how it should be done. The message was clear: between now and the time we sail, I'd better brush up on my splicing.

I set out to weave the net strands into the bolt rope, slowly working my way forward, while the Captain and Sean went off to other tasks.

Left on my own, I marveled at the place where I was, out in front of the ship, 25 feet above the water. What, I wondered, will it be like out here when we're at sea? If the ship were pitching, the bowsprit might well dip below the waves and send sheets of water back on crew members out here working the foresails, and I felt a tingle of excitement. At the same time, I knew it would be prudent to stay as dry and warm as possible under such circumstances, and I remembered with fondness the neoprene gloves I'd bought, though getting them off quickly when you needed to could be hard, and what to do with them when you weren't using them could be a problem. While thinking these thoughts, I nearly lost my Irish cap in the wind, and this was a moderately calm day with the ship in her berth.

The bays and headlands on the west coast of Ireland face the open sea, so the weather, fresh off the Atlantic, is raw and untamed. One day may be mist and drizzle; the next, dark overcast with a howling 50-knot wind; and the third, clear sunshine with a gentle breeze. At Fenit, work on the ship was always at the mercy of the weather.

The following day was clear and sunny, and the Captain intended to make the most of it. "Today we'll do some chores up in the rigging," he told Sean and me.

Look up at the rigging of the *Jeanie Johnston* and you see a confusing array of ropes and cables-- lines, sheets, halyards, braces, brails, stays, ratlines, shrouds, gaskets and lifts, along with a few others I've forgotten. The Captain knows them all by heart.

"First stop is up the foremast. There are a couple of blocks we've got to change." I'd never climbed ratlines, but there they were right before me. "Put your feet on the ropes and your hands on the shrouds," said the Captain. I did, and found it surprisingly easy.

The ratlines have spliced loops at either end, and the loops are lashed to the shrouds. There's plenty of give when you step on them, but they feel sturdy and solid. Up we went to a location between the fore course yard and the fore topsail yard, the replacement blocks tied to our safety belts. We clipped our tethers to a handy cable and went to work.

Our first chore was to remove the existing blocks from their shackles and replace them with the ones we'd brought up. That done, the Captain left Sean and me to complete the job. Sean freed the deck ends of the lines and fed them up through their fair leads while I removed the lines from the old blocks, fed them through the new ones and handed them back to Sean, who fed them back through the fair leads and secured them on the deck.

I quickly learned two things about working aloft. Sliding between the stays and shrouds as I shifted my body from one side of the mast to the other, a back pocket of my jeans, bulging with my wallet, caught on one of the shrouds. Lesson No.1: Empty your pockets before going aloft; keep as slim a profile as possible. Lesson No. 2 was one all sailors know: "On a boat, anything that can snag will snag." I looked at my wristwatch and realized that almost anything in the rigging could reach out, snag the latch and fling my watch overboard. If you don't want to lose them, leave wallets, watches and anything else of value below decks.

There was a third lesson too, and I learned it the hard way. As I went back down the ratlines, the old block I'd tied to my safety belt slipped off and clattered down onto the deck.

Fortunately no one was in the vicinity, but before we left the ship, Michael O'Boyle expressed his displeasure to the Captain and the Captain passed it on to me. Now I know why workmen on the deck wear their hard hats. I don't know what knot I'd used, but from now on, anything on my safety belt would be secured with a round turn and two half hitches.

There was still daylight and sunshine left, so we followed the Captain on to his next chore, which took us up the mizzen mast. A metal collar around the mast was held in place by a slightly corroded bolt. The fact that the Captain had spotted this was quite revealing. It meant that he must inspect the rigging frequently and minutely. Actually, he was in a position no captain savors. He couldn't sail his ship because it was still crawling with workmen. So he had thrown himself into the process, coordinating decisions on the finishing touches-- and checking every detail.

The corroded bolt was under tension, and Sean couldn't turn it. "Tom, get that small clamp down in the work shed, will you?" I was relieved that he'd asked me, and not the younger crew member, to climb down the rigging and back up again. I was eager to prove that I could do what was expected of me.

But I got more than I'd bargained for. The clamp was too small. "We'll need that big one," said the Captain. Down the ratlines again, off the ship and into the shed. I found the clamp, and it was a giant-- two feet long and it must have weighed 30 pounds. "Want me to come down and get it?" he asked from aloft when I reappeared. "No, I'll bring it up," I said. It was too heavy to tie to my safety belt, so I carried it in one hand while I hauled myself up the rigging with the other. He took it without comment, but I felt I'd passed some kind of test, and it was a good feeling.

A moment later, though, a breeze sprang up and I looked out to sea. Here in her berth, the ship was virtually motionless. Who couldn't climb the rigging on a mast that was as unmoving as a tree in the forest? When the ship was in her element, and everything was in motion, it would be a different story. And that thought quickly brought me back to earth.

After my day in the rigging, my body knew it had done some work, and I laughed quietly to myself as I recalled writing to Mike Forwood six months earlier, suggesting that the passengers (I didn't realize then we'd all be working crew) would need exercise on such a long sea voyage, and that a rowing machine or some such device would be useful. He had replied succinctly, "Don't worry. At the end of the day, you won't need any exercise." Now I understood.

After a few days of interviews, consultations and deck chores, I felt I was getting to know the ship, at least in a cursory fashion. What I had learned, though, was only a drop in the ocean compared with Mike Forwood's store of knowledge. Yet even he had much to learn, and he couldn't learn it there at the dock. When the voyage got underway, part of the adventure-- for all of us-- would be getting to know the ship herself.

In the Age of Exploration, the mystery was always what lay beyond the horizon. The venturing ship was usually as familiar as an old piece of furniture. Columbus's caravels, for example, had been the sturdy little workhorses of the seas for generations. Captains and crews knew their every nuance and were not likely to be surprised by the ship in any circumstances.

There's no mystery any more about what lies "beyond the gray Azores, beyond the Gates of Hercules." We'd be sailing to a world we know as well as the one we leave behind. But we'd be discovering new things about the ship from the moment we stepped aboard her.

"The ship is a standard design of her time," said the Captain. "Nothing remarkable or different about the design. But we're not of her time, so in that sense we'll be exploring what she will and won't do, how she reacts to different sea and weather conditions."

Unfortunately, no plans or photographs of the original *Jeanie Johnston* have been found, only a survey report that lists its principal dimensions and the materials from which it was built. For the rest, the designer had to turn to a study of similar ships of the day. But even if we had a precise record of how the original *Jeanie Johnston* behaved under every condition, we couldn't necessarily apply it to the new *Jeanie Johnston*.

The replica ship has tons of lead and steel the original didn't have-- bulkheads, engines, generators and tanks. Bolted to her oak keel is a steel box section filled with lead, and a steel keelson runs the length of the ship. Four steel bulkheads divide the hull into watertight compartments, and the oak beams are connected with steel knees. Even the deckhouses, for reasons of fire safety, are made of steel faced with iroko, a subtropical hardwood.

Her builders calculated the center of gravity of the wooden hull and then decided-- within the limits of practicality-- where to place the tanks, ballast and other heavy items. Even so, there will be more buoyancy amidships and lots of weight in the aft end, where the engines are located.

"She won't be an exact replica in terms of her sailing characteristics," said the Captain. "We can guess that the weight distribution will be somewhat different from the original."

As long as she sat in her berth, there wasn't much he could learn about her performance under sail. "I'd guess that she'll turn out to be fairly stiff," he said ("Stiff" is a good thing if you want stability. It's a sailing term applied to a boat or ship that doesn't heel excessively under sail). A stiff ship, said Mike, is good in bad weather but usually uncomfortable for the crew. A tender ship is the opposite-- bad news in bad weather but a more comfortable ride for the crew as it comes back to the upright position with a slow roll. He was hoping for a compromise but would know for sure only when the ship gets her sea trials.

When Captain Jack Aubrey, the hero of Patrick O'Brian's sea novels, steps aboard a new ship, his finely-tuned antennae are all aquiver. He thirsts for knowledge: "He had been on fire to know how she handled ever since he had set eyes on the *Polychrest*. She had the strangest motion as she rose to the swell, a kind of twist to her roll that he had never known before."

Jack paces back and forth, his hands behind his back and his mind working overtime. "The figure of the *Polychrest* was as clear in his mind as if she had been a model held up to a lamp, and he mentally studied her reaction to the creeping influence of the tide and the lateral thrust of the wind."

Captain Forwood is also a man deeply experienced in the ways of tall ships, and he was thirsting for knowledge of how the *Jeanie Johnston* would respond to the helm, how much leeway she would make when on the wind, how easy it would be to put her about. Those are all points of knowledge he would learn when the ship had her sea trials, and when the crew eventually came aboard, if we were curious enough and sailors enough, we would be eager to learn those lessons from him.

Other questions might prove more difficult to answer. One thing I wanted to try to fathom before I left Tralee was why the projected timing for the ship's completion and maiden voyage had been so far off.

The delays had affected many people. Irish/American communities along the US eastern seaboard had planned festivals, art shows and other cultural events to welcome the *Jeanie Johnston*. All had to be canceled or tenuously rescheduled. Crew members for whom the voyage coincided with a window of opportunity-- a sabbatical or accrued vacation time-- had dropped out. Captain Forwood's permanent crew, at one point almost fully assembled, had dwindled to himself and engineer Michael O'Carroll, while others took part-time jobs or went back to school until the *Jeanie Johnston* had a dependable schedule.

Everyone knew the surface reasons-- shipments of bad wood, a scarcity of skilled shipwrights, problems at the launching, weather delays, the complexities of meeting 21st century maritime standards. But couldn't some of these have been foreseen and planned for?

The problem went deeper, and after talking with everyone on all sides, I believed I could finally put my finger on it. There were two opposing cultures at work on the ship-- the managers and the builders. The managers had their sights on fulfilling the expectations of the sponsors, paying off the debt, reaping the glory. The builders were intent on just one thing-- creating the perfect ship. Why hadn't the two communicated more fruitfully? Perhaps they speak different languages. The managers' language is compounded of objectives and schedules; the builders, of ancient wisdom and inborn knowledge. Maybe it became too easy, under pressure, to come up with a guess when a question really had no answer.

Some decisions may have been political rather than practical. The ship was nowhere near ready by her original sailing date, April of 2000, but her hull was complete, so it was decided to launch her at that time. This provided a grand occasion for dignitaries but gave the rest of the world a false impression. Moreover, it complicated the ensuing work greatly. At Blennerville, where the ship was born, work had progressed under a giant shelter, secure from the worst of the weather. Fenit, the deep water port to which she was moved, is totally unprotected and lacking in many port facilities, so the work was slowed appreciably.

From the beginning, the intent had been to build a real ship that could sail the oceans of the world, and that meant meeting the stringent international safety standards that apply to all modern deep sea passenger ships. An earlier Irish replica ship, built by the Kennedy Foundation, sits at the dock in Waterford, where she must live out her life as a local museum ship because she was not built to those standards and so can never be certified for an ocean passage. It is likely that the *Jeanie Johnston*'s builders did not fully comprehend at the outset the complexity of accommodating 21st century safety standards in the limited structure of a 19th century ship.

What many apparently failed to understand, too, was that the builders were embarked on their own voyage of discovery. With only a survey to guide him, the designer of the replica ship had provided basic drawings but virtually no details. In essence, the builders were making things up as they went along, and their decisions became more complicated as they progressed from the gross tasks of framing and planking to the finer dimensions of detail work and operating systems.

80

When Captain Forwood arrived on the scene, he secured the services of a well-known naval architect who volunteered as a draftsman, fleshing out the details of the ship's spaces and systems on a computer. Thus the design and construction were proceeding neck and neck, one informing the other in the process.

Whatever the problems, though, the ship would rise above them all. At least that's what Turlough O'Connell told me, and I found his rationale compelling. Turlough, who then worked at the project's New York office, believed that the ship, and the vision that brought it to life, were greater than anything that could happen along the way-- greater than the delays and mistakes, greater than the petty human failings that trailed in its wake. In the end, he felt, the ship would emerge triumphant over all because it is a grand vision and a worthy one.

Listening to Turlough, and now seeing the ship, I'd had my faith restored.

CHAPTER 7
Secret Lives Of A Tall Ship

"When she's finished, she'll be the most sophisticated wooden ship afloat," John Griffin had told me on the first day of my Tralee visit. He was leaning back in his chair, obviously pleased with the thought. At the time, I had taken his statement with a grain of salt. There were, after all, hundreds of tall ships around the world-- the directory of The American Sail Training Association pictured and described them all-- and it seemed to be stretching credibility to say the *Jeanie Johnston* would be that different from the best of the worldwide fleet.

By the end of my Tralee stay, I found his claim not at all hard to believe.

One way to assess her unique qualities is to compare her with the average run of 19th century ships, including the original Jeanie. When the *Jeanie Johnston* sailed from Ireland, she would be commemorating not only the original *Jeanie*, which plied the Atlantic in the 1850s, but also all the less wholesome famine ships that carried thousands of Irish emigrants to the shores of America. This ship would cross the same ocean they did, but almost everything else would be vastly different.

Not many of today's wooden ships, for example-- and certainly not the original *Jeanie Johnston* or any of her 19th century contemporaries-- were built with watertight compartments. Four steel bulkheads divide the *Jeanie Johnston*'s hull into five such compartments. Unlike those on the ill-fated *Titanic*, they extend all the way up to seal off the inner spaces of the hull completely from one another. If a giant whale were to ram the ship-- like the monster that rammed and sank the 19th century whale ship *Essex* in the Pacific and inspired Herman Melville to write *Moby Dick*--only one compartment would flood. And that assumes the whale would have enough ramming power to rupture the ship's four- to five-inch planking.

Even if she ran head-on into trouble, or suffered a rear-end collision, the effects would be muted by specially-reinforced sections-- the "forward collision bulkhead" and the "after collision bulkhead."

The ship's backup systems are also highly advanced. Its two generators would run most of the time during the voyage to keep the deep freeze going, though Captain Forwood admitted they might be turned off from time to time "so we can experience nothing but the sounds of sailing." If the generators should ever fail, or the ship be rendered powerless because of grounding, an emergency generator would spring into action to drive the two fire pumps and bilge pumps (one each in the engine room and tank room).

Serious precautions have been taken against fire, with a CO_2 system in the engine room, hydrants throughout the ship, hand extinguishers and breathing apparatus. The deck is fire-insulated, and the deck houses, for fire safety, are made of steel that is insulated and then clad with tongue-and-groove wood. Besides, all members of the professional crew would have fire-fighting and survival certificates.

On 19th century ships, there were no generators or deep freeze units. Some ships had fire pumps, on others wash-deck hoses were pressed into use, and many deck fires were fought simply by passing buckets of water from hand to hand. There were no CO_2 systems or fire extinguishers.

Perhaps the most notable operational difference between the modern *Jeanie Johnston* and her 19th century counterparts is her highly efficient auxiliary power plant, though I must reassure sailing purists that it is there only for emergency use at sea and for maneuvering through restrictive coastal and river waters when she is on her tour of US and Canadian ports.

When she called on Washington, she would need to travel more than 50 miles from Chesapeake Bay up the Potomac River to her dock-- probably in Alexandria, Virginia. In the days of pure sail, such a maneuver would have required the highest skills of seamanship and freedom from time schedules. It would have been accomplished by making use of the tide and the sails in an intricate interplay of moves, occasionally setting the anchor to swing the ship into a more favorable position with respect to the wind. When the tide no longer sufficed, the crew probably would have taken to the ship's boats and put their backs to the oars to tow her the rest of the way. To travel in that painstaking manner through the river's twistings and turnings could have taken days.

With her two 280 horsepower Caterpillar diesels, rated at 2,200 rpm, the *Jeanie Johnston* would be capable of doing up to 10 knots on power alone, getting her from the mouth of the Potomac to Alexandria in a matter of hours.

Just as tedious as navigating a tidal estuary was the business of moving a sailing ship into or out of her dock, or from a protected harbor to the open sea. It was often done by warping, and "warp speed" today means something entirely different, thanks to science fiction, than it did in the 19th century.

A vessel was warped around the port with the help of heavy posts, called dolphins, set along the edges of the channels. Sailors carried hawsers out by ship's boat and fastened them to the dolphins; then the crew aboard the ship hauled on the hawsers to move the ship ever so slowly from one dolphin to another.

The *Jeanie Johnston* would not only have power; she would also have the maneuverability to virtually turn on a dime as the

84

need arose or edge adroitly up to her dock with all the aplomb of a modern power boat. Running through the forward part of her hull, from one side to another, is a small-diameter open tunnel. At its center is a bow thruster-- an electric-powered reversible motor with a propeller that draws water in from one side of the ship and pushes it out the other to move the ship's bow from side to side, giving her a great advantage in tight spots. When the time came to navigate through canal locks on her way to the Great Lakes, the bow thruster would surely be a boon for Captain Forwood and his crew.

More dramatic than anything else, though, are the advances that would make life easier and more comfortable for the people living and working aboard.

From the decks of their ships, the poor Irish emigrants of the 19th century could see "water, water, everywhere," but often enough there was not a drop to drink. To get their daily ration, they had to line up on deck whenever the mates decided to open the casks. Sometimes the rationing would be capriciously stopped, and many had to wait until the next day or the day after to fill their cups or jugs. Water was always in meager supply.

The *Jeanie Johnston* would have water resources the old skippers could never have dreamed of. The ship would carry 12 tons (more than 3,000 gallons) of water in three tanks. Her water maker would produce four tons or 4,000 liters of water (more than 1,000 gallons) a day. It's estimated that the daily use of water would be about 500 gallons. There would be more than enough to drink whenever anyone wants it.

How did the Irish emigrants keep clean? Mostly they didn't. With water so scarce and precious, how could you waste it for washing when you barely had enough to slake your thirst? As a result the air below decks was foul and fetid-- a perfect breeding ground for disease.

On the *Jeanie Johnston*, crew members would be able to step into a refreshing shower when they needed to, and laundry facilities would keep their clothing clean and fresh.

Sanitary facilities on the old ships were as simple as they could be. Passengers used a bucket below decks, carried it up on deck and dumped its contents overboard. The sanitary system had a simple name: "Bucket and Chuck It."

The *Jeanie Johnston*'s waste system is highly sophisticated, employing the latest technology presently used on ships and airplanes. At its heart is a Super Trident sewage treatment plant, capable of handling a daily sewage flow of more than 6,000 liters. While the crew went about their work above deck, millions of patient bacteria would be absorbing nutrients and turning waste into biodegraded residue. The system is certified and accepted by the US Coast Guard for use on non-US flag vessels operating in US waters.

Food aboard the famine ships was a mixed bag at best. In the first years of the famine, the British Passengers' Acts required ships to provide each passenger each week with a total of seven pounds of food-- bread, biscuit, flour, rice, oatmeal or potatoes. But a pound of food a day was little more than a starvation ration, and those who could afford it carried their own rations with them.

Even so, it was no picnic. The ship provided crude boxes lined with bricks in which passengers were supposed to cook their food on deck. An apprentice seaman called Jack in the Shrouds climbed the rigging with a jug of water to douse the flames when they were through-- or when he thought they should be. When the weather was rough, as it might be for days on end, no cooking was allowed.

Now read this description from the new *Jeanie*'s Crew Information Book: "The menu content is to be wholesome, well balanced and sufficient in quantity to sustain the needs of very active and hungry young people and the expectations of adults. The raw materials are to be of the finest quality, the cooking and presentation of the highest standard. The highest codes of hygiene are to be observed in the storage, preparation and cooking environment."

The "cooking environment" is an all-stainless steel galley that would be the envy of any hotel chef, though a little less spacious than he might require. Here's the menu: "Breakfast: Full cooked meal of minimum four items preceded by cereal, porridge or fruit, followed by toast, preserves, coffee and tea. Lunch: Soup with cheese or salad, pasta or rice dishes, potato topped pies, etc. Followed by fresh fruit, bread, hot and cold beverage. Dinner: Full cooked main course of meat, fish, potatoes and two vegetables with gravy or a sauce, plus dessert, bread, coffee and tea. Soup may replace dessert. Breaks: Beverages hot or cold and biscuits, etc."

But all these facts about the ship's construction, propulsion system and maneuverability, and her onboard water, sanitary and feeding facilities, relate to only one aspect of the *Jeanie Johnston*-- her sailing life.

In that life, she would perform as any sailing vessel does, carrying a live-aboard crew who handle the sails, do the chores and navigate her to her desired destination. That's a standard description of any tall ship and is nothing new. But the *Jeanie Johnston* is not a "standard" ship. In addition to her sailing life, she would have two secret lives, neither to be fully revealed to the public until she reaches American and Canadian waters.

Her builders have described her as a ship of three modes: (1) the standard sailing mode, with a working crew; (2) the museum mode, when all reminders of the 21st century disappear from her decks and below-deck spaces; and (3) the corporate mode, when she becomes the perfect setting for a power breakfast or a corporate awards banquet.

John Griffin had let me in on the bag of tricks that would turn her into a museum. "Come, let me show you something," he said with a sly smile as we sat in his office in the Ashe Memorial Hall in Tralee. The building also houses the Tralee Tourist Office, the Kerry-the-Kingdom Museum and the stunning permanent exhibit of medieval life called Geraldine Tralee. John is the prime mover behind all these entities.

I followed him down three flights of stairs and we seated ourselves in a "time car," which, like a fun-house ride, transported
us back to 1450 A.D., when Tralee was ruled by the Anglo-
Norman FitzGerald family.

In no time at all, we were on the main street of the medieval
town, moving slowly past the houses and tradesmen's shops of
a bustling little market community.

Life-size human figures-- a leatherworker and a blacksmith
at work, a fisherwoman peddling her wares-- were startling not
only because of the utterly lifelike positions in which the display builders had caught them, but also because each was a dis-
tinct personality, with facial features that you would swear must
be those of a real person.

Moving past timber-framed houses with thatched roofs, the
parish church, the Dominican friary and the castle, we saw people shopping and chatting, animals, wagons and chickens peck-
ing in the dirt. Travelers, standing on a street corner, were apparently asking for directions. Through an open door, we could
see a kitchen table set for a meal. A woman in a second-story
window is caught in the act of dumping a bucket of slop into the
street below.

Not only could we see all this; we could also hear it and smell
it. The blacksmith's hammer rang against iron, and the smell of
the leatherman's product was clearly perceptible as we went past
his shop. Dogs barked and chickens squawked.

Obviously, no expense had been spared to create this tableau
in time. A nationally famed archaeologist had searched castles,
churches and tombs all across Ireland for clues to medieval construction and data on clothing and crafts. The Project had
reached out to Dublin's world-renowned theater district for set
designers and model makers.

Even the Vatican Library was impressed. In a preface to the
museum's illustrated brochure, its Prefect, Leonard E. Boyle
O.P., wrote that "the distant past... had been teased back into
life. Drawing brilliantly on survivals from all over Ireland, and

calling on many crafts and disciplines, the designers have re-created a typical port-town of medieval Ireland. It is the first of its kind in Ireland and a splendid example of a marriage of imagination and scholarship."

As we stepped out of the time car, John Griffin was ready with his punch line. With a broad smile, he said, "What you see here is the kind of exhibit you'll see on the *Jeanie Johnston*. The same talent that produced this 15th century market town will produce the interior of a 19th century emigrant ship. When you board the ship, you'll step into the 19th century, and each step will be a new experience. It will be informative, educational and entertaining. You'll be learning history, but the experience will be enjoyable."

There would be no descriptive panels, signs or video dis-plays-- nothing that would not have been seen aboard the origi-nal *Jeanie Johnston* in the 1850s. A tour guide would brief visitors at several stations, but mostly they would be on their own, surrounded by an exhibit of living history that would com-municate in its own way-- by sight, sound and smell.

They would enter that 19th century world the moment they approached the ship's gangplank. There, sitting on top of a trunk, surrounded by packing cases, crates and barrels, would appear the figure of an emaciated, dejected young child, staring at the ground. Here is the speech they might hear from the guide who greeted them:

"Welcome aboard. For the next few minutes pretend you are an emigrant, boarding this ship for a journey almost beyond your imagination. Because of the famine, you are leaving be-hind everything you know and love and are about to sail across the Atlantic on a two-month voyage to enable you to start a new life in America or Canada. You have with you your worldly goods, which amount to not much more than you can carry, and in many cases you have only the clothes you stand up in. The noise will be unbelievable as everyone pushes and jostles, fami-lies are separated from one another, the crew try to maintain some kind of order, and on shore loved ones wail and shout as you prepare to leave them forever."

As they went below decks and through the ship's storage area, visitors would pass an animatronic display of a stowaway. The lid of a barrel rises slowly, a small child peers out briefly and the lid closes again. On the wall, a poster appeals for information about stowaways.

The heart-wrenching fact is that small children were often smuggled aboard emigrant vessels inside luggage or barrels, and it may be illuminating to try to imagine the conditions that would move parents to resort to such a drastic and uncertain escape mechanism for their offspring.

In the main exhibition space-- the large 'tweendecks area with crew bunks along both sides and a long dining table in the middle-- the lighting would be dim, simulating candles and lanterns. The number of heads and feet sticking out from under blankets on each bunk would dramatize the number of people-- probably about 80-- crammed into space on the original *Jeanie Johnston* that would be occupied by 16 crew members on today's ship.

Visitors might see a figure of a young mother nursing a newborn infant; a passenger eating, with some distaste, moldy ship's biscuits and cheese; a sailor carrying a pitcher of water. Other exhibits might include a wooden-framed canvas latrine; crates of chickens and vegetables stored on top of the deckhouse; and a decktop cooking stove.

"As a passenger," their guide would tell them, "you would be expected to cook for yourself and your family. The stove was on deck, and you had to take your turn. That meant that your main meal of the day could be at 6 o'clock in the morning, 6 at night, or any time in between. If the weather was too rough, you would probably miss your turn and your family would simply go hungry that day."

Visitors would be made aware that an 1850s Atlantic crossing was primitive at worst and roughing it at best. The bunks, in fact, were so roughly made that when the passengers were discharged and a cargo, probably of lumber, was taken aboard for the return trip to Ireland, they were simply torn out and burned.

When the ship wasn't a museum, she would be sailing from port to port or serving as a unique nautical venue for a corporate event. Shifting from sailing mode to museum mode to corporate mode and then back again would require logistical programming that few, if any, tall ships have ever had to deal with; and that, in turn, would give the Captain a set of challenges no master of a 19th Century ship ever faced.

The secret to quick changes would be in the "tween deck," the main below-deck living area, with its bunks and central table.

When the crew was aboard, they would sleep in the bunks and eat at the table. In museum mode, the bunks and table would be part of the exhibit, along with the life-size figures of 19th century emigrants, concealed lights and speakers. In corporate mode, bunk compartment partitions would be removed, the top bunks would slide down to form seats, and the table would expand to seat 66.

At dock in the US and Canada, the *Jeanie Johnston* might live all three lives in the course of a single day. "You could have a corporate breakfast in the morning," said shipwright foreman Ciaran O'Regan, "then a museum between 10 am and 4 pm, then a corporate dinner, then change back to the sailing mode late in the evening. When the ship is in the US, she'll be going non-stop."

A new crew would come aboard for each port-to-port leg of the voyage, and that would further complicate things. On a typical sailing between ports, the crew might report aboard at noon, sign in, get basic training, go aloft, learn sail handling, then sleep aboard. The ship departs the next morning, and once out of port, the crew practices tacking and wearing, then the ship sails for the next port, arriving late and lying offshore.

The following morning, the crew makes the switch from sailing mode to museum mode, the ship docks, the crew departs, officials come aboard for formal greetings and a tour of the ship, and by noon the museum is opened to the public.

For the Captain and his officers, all this means a lot of juggling, along with precision timing. Partitions would have to be taken down and stowed, then put back in place again for the next act. Life-size "emigrants" must be removed from lockers, placed on benches or bunks, then stowed away again. On deck, the ship's modern rescue boat and life rafts would have to be concealed when the ship is in 19th century mode, then redeployed for the 21st century. Crew members would have to be signed in, trained and signed out. Liaison must be maintained with shore-side facilities that would follow the ship from port to port to set up and man a dockside pavilion with historical, genealogical and economics exhibits.

In short, the ship's time in the US and Canada would be long on administrative detail and short on oceangoing adventure. Her time at sea would be quite different.

When the *Jeanie Johnston* arrived fresh from her transatlantic voyage, the voyage crew would depart, somewhat reluctantly perhaps, but certain that we'd enjoyed the best she had to offer-- the beauty and stimulation of pure sail. We would also have had the unique experience of living and working in challenging conditions with a small group of people who will remember one another for the rest of their lives almost as vividly as members of their own families. Of the ship's three lives, the sailing life I hoped to live with her was surely the best.

Meanwhile, it was time to resume the waiting game, though this time in a somewhat improved climate. I am not a patient person by nature; in the business world, one of my favorite mottoes had been "Do It Now!" But when dealing with leprechauns, one must realize that the rules are not only changed; they are discarded altogether. The result had brought a certain disorderliness to my life.

I had packed and unpacked and then partially packed again. Items whose shelf life tends to be limited-- like portioned-out daily vitamins or photo film-- would by now have been sitting in my duffle bag for six months if I hadn't decided to gradually use them up. Now the stores had to be replenished. And since I didn't monitor my packing area-- in a guest bedroom-- every day, or even every week, I tended to forget what was there. Wouldn't it be a good idea, I thought one day, to take some throwaway safety razors in case my electric shaver fails to function? When I went to stow them, I found a supply already there, sparked by the same thought months earlier.

While the waiting was no more pleasant than it had been, it was now at least a more informed wait. I had seen the ship, spent memorable time aboard her and made a start at "learning the ropes." My week with Captain Mike Forwood, Michael O'Carroll and John Griffin had been an invaluable experience, and it had made me an insider of sorts. Now that we had met, done some deck chores together, gone up and down the ratlines a few times and toasted one another over a pint of Guinness, I felt that I had been accepted, and that any lingering thoughts about limitations imposed by my age had been put to rest. Best of all, there was now a human factor. When I wrote, called or e-mailed, I could picture the live person at the other end. I understood their hopes and frustrations, and they understood mine.

My personal contact with the ship itself had made a huge difference, too. The more I came to know the *Jeanie Johnston*, the more convinced I was that she was unique and special. It wasn't just what she stood for; it wasn't just the Irish connection via my grandmother; it wasn't just the way she always tantalized me, beckoning me on and then at the last moment moving out of reach. It was all of those and something more-- something I couldn't define that had given her a place of almost mythic stature in my consciousness.

Like it or not, the *Jeanie Johnston* had become an integral part of my life.

93

CHAPTER 8
"The Project Has Been Abandoned"

As we approached the end of the year 2000, I was reminded of the scene a year earlier, when Marie and I had toasted my forthcoming millennial voyage on the *Jeanie Johnston*.

Here we were, almost a year later, and the voyage was still off somewhere in the Irish mists. Months earlier, Captain Forwood had spoken of a January departure, and during my visit to the ship in October I had assumed that was our target date, but there had been no mention of any timing since, and there still was no official sailing date.

Gus, my Ancient Hibernian friend, said there wasn't much talk about the ship in AOH circles any more. "Millennial," said another friend of a waggish bent, "means they'll do it sometime in this millennium." I might have reminded him that the real millennial year was just dawning on January 1, 2001, and that the world had jumped the gun with its celebrations a year earlier, but I withheld comment. I wasn't buying into his cynicism. Somehow or other, I still had faith, though it had precious little solid basis.

The hope for a January sailing apparently had been fraying at the edges even while I visited the ship, and well before the end of the millennial year it unraveled altogether. The troubles had surfaced earlier when it was revealed that the Project had incurred a IR£2 million cost overrun. The Irish government had stepped in to fund the overrun charges, and at the same time the

County government of Kerry had underwritten a IR£2 million bank loan to complete the ship.

As part of the agreement that rescued the Project financially, the *Jeanie Johnston* directors were required to develop a new management plan that would include a rigorous review of the costs already incurred and those remaining as well as a realistic completion date and a precise description of how the North American voyage would be accomplished. The Irish government advanced the Project £700,000 on account but refused to part with the remaining £1.3 million until they came up with a satisfactory plan.

As soon as I returned from Ireland, I called Turlough McConnell in the Project's New York office to discuss the *Jeanie Johnston* newsletter. He was to be my stateside contact on the newsletter, and it probably would be produced by his office. Turlough was on his way to a major strategy meeting in Tralee-- a three-day conference at which the new management plan was to be presented and discussed. He called me on November 14, shortly after his return, and his message was not a welcome one.

"We spent a week analyzing the voyage," he said, "and I am not sure where we stand going forward." The Tralee County Board had assumed a policy-making role in the Project and it was not yet clear what their reactions were to the plan. There were also some management changes. The newsletter was the least urgent matter on anyone's agenda at the moment. And most disheartening of all was Turlough's news that, while there was no public announcement to the effect, the management document now projected a March sailing at the earliest.

My experience to date with the *Jeanie Johnston* had been that when bad news arrived it usually came in twos or threes. Now I was waiting not only for a sailing date but also for approval of the newsletter proposal, and neither was forthcoming. I asked Turlough a few days later if he was hearing the same "deafening silence" that assailed my ears. He was no better off, though it was a different sense that was affected. "I am totally in the dark," he responded. Then, to drop the final shoe, an email from Mike Forwood told me the weather in Tralee had been "dreadful," which surely meant there was little work being done on the ship.

Murphy, the promulgator of the law that bears his name, might well have added that whenever anything is clarified, it is always clarified for the worse. When I finally was able to reach a member of the ship's management group in early November, he told me the finalized plan called for a mid-April to early May sailing date, with May more likely than April, to arrive in Washington in June. That would be a full year from the time I had originally expected to fly to Ireland, board the ship and sail off on our adventure.

I could imagine the turmoil in Tralee. With members of the County Council now involved, along with the original management group of the Jeanie Johnston Company, there were many hands stirring the pot, and perhaps not all in the same direction. Getting a firm answer to a question or a positive commitment to an activity like the newsletter proved more elusive every day.

Frustration finally drove me to action. I emailed Tralee and offered to turn to immediately and write the first issue of the newsletter based on information I had gathered during my visit; proposed that it be produced in New York and suggested that even if there were no budget, Turlough McConnell and I would find the funds somewhere in the US to get the job done. There had been no news on the Project's web site for months, and its North American constituents were badly in need of cultivating if their interest in the ship were to be kept alive. But though Turlough and I took turns badgering the Tralee management, there still were no decisions forthcoming.

The best information on the local situation was now showing up on the "focuskerry" web site, operated in Tralee by a woman named Helen Ryle. I had established contact with Helen several months earlier, met her over a pint of Guinness when I visited the ship, and we were now regular email pen pals. Helen, a resident of Blennerville, had become interested in the *Jeanie Johnston* in the course of driving past the shipyard every day on her way to work. She had taught herself how to construct a web site for her family-run shop in Tralee and decided to devote a portion of the site to the *Jeanie Johnston* Project because, she said, "I think the Project is inspirational and the ship itself is a beautiful piece of workmanship." She wanted, she said, "to provide a pictorial chronicle of shipyard events for posterity."

Helen, who had been posting stories and photographs since the ship's beginning, had also conceived the ideas of having schoolchildren write about their impressions of the Project and offering postcards based on photos of the ship. She had proved to be a cannily effective communicator, and the philosophy she expressed on her web site had impressed me as some of the finest words I had read about the *Jeanie Johnston*:

"We have received many messages from people who empathize with the spirit of the *Jeanie Johnston* voyage, its roots and ideals. Remembering and rejoining with one's roots from past generations, and a sense of building on one's heritage to forge a stronger future, this is what the *Jeanie Johnston* embodies. I think that, whatever the delays and trepidations which have beset the project, the spirit of Jeanie will survive and triumph, that she will be met with much affection and generosity in the US and Canada, and in hard financial terms will meet her building costs and surpass them from sponsorship, revenue from visitors and corporate events.

"I also hope that people who visit and support Jeanie will take a little time to stand aside from their daily busy lives to honour their heritage and remember their ancestors whose courage brought them to the shores of the New World. When you touch the *Jeanie Johnston*, the beauty of the wood and the excellence of the craftsmanship transports you to a bygone age, one that many feel is worth remembering."

In mid-December, Helen's web site reported that "the Kerry

coast has been battered by storms and gale-force winds these past few months, whilst the *Jeanie Johnston* lies at her moorings at Fenit pier, continuing to be fitted out. In the three months September-November, we have experienced 33 inches of rain-fall, over half the annual average."

Photographs showed the ship with tarpaulins covering the deck houses to protect them and the workmen from the weather. "The continuing overrun in time." she reported, "has meant continuing overrun in costs, and the final total of building the Jeanie is expected to approach £10 million." The leprechauns, it seemed, were pulling out all the stops.

It would be difficult, under these circumstances, to project a firm sailing date even if an exact work schedule existed. But it didn't, as I had discovered in Tralee.

So the Project was bedeviled by uncertainty about the amount of work needed to complete the ship, by an assortment of management changes and now by the worst of an Irish winter, which at best is nothing to be grateful for. The response of the Project's leaders was essentially to remain silent, lest they stir up more controversy. No reports were issued, questions were mostly unanswered and the web site went virtually dead.

"Your many supporters here in the US are eager for news of the *Jeanie Johnston*," I told them, "and there is a great deal you can tell them-- how the ship is being built, her various mechanical systems, her three modes (crewed, museum and corporate), who the crew will be, how they will be trained, how the ship will be navigated, etc. All this can be based on solid, authoritative information now available and has nothing to do with the sailing date or the itinerary, which are yet to be decided."

But those words merely described what might be done. The end product-- the actual newsletter-- was beginning to assemble in my head. The stories started writing themselves, almost spontaneously, with opening paragraphs and potential headlines floating into place. Within two days, I had created a computer format for a four-page newsletter, written all the stories for the first issue and printed out a dummy with spaces for photographs. The newsletter would be called *"Grand Voyage."* I was especially proud of a front-page story headlined *JJ Is Perfect Symbol for the Celtic Tiger.* "When CBS decided to feature the booming Irish economy on 60 Minutes II," it began, "it could find no more fitting symbol for Ireland's success than the ship that has become the pride of Ireland, the *Jeanie Johnston.*" Other stories described the ship's three modes; the genealogical project; the men-- John Griffin, Michael O'Boyle and the O'Regan brothers-- who had brought the dream to life; and the people, including the young Trenton carpenter, whose lives had been changed by their contact with the *Jeanie Johnston.*

Wasn't this putting the cart before the horse? Assuredly, it was. No one had asked me to write a newsletter; no one had even responded to my proposal. But I was so impatient to get on with the voyage that I had to do something, and my proposed newsletter was there to do.

"You're trying to will the ship to completion," said Marie, and that reminded me of a zen story about a man who was so impatient for the spring flowers to come up that he took to pulling on them to make them grow faster. The moral, that some things can't be rushed, wasn't lost on me, though it didn't deter me either.

On New Year's Day, 2001, I sent my editorial package off to Ireland, by both email and fax, to be sure it would arrive safely. But other than the phrase "good job" dropped here and there in the weeks following, nothing ever came of it.

The calendar was now my enemy because there was no way I could use it to plan other facets of our lives. My alma mater, Rutgers, was offering an eight-day Alumni College in Tuscany, a prospect Marie and I found highly attractive. The dates were April 25 to May 3. The last word I'd had from Tralee on the voyage was mid-April to early May.

"I'd appreciate your honest opinion on this," I wrote to Mike Forwood. "When do you think I will need to report to the ship? If there is any chance that the timing for this Italian trip wouldn't work, I wouldn't want to risk it, but then the ship's schedule seems to be slipping again, and I thought it would be worth asking about."

Mike's reply reflected his own frustration and uncertainty. He had been on a nine-day port tour in Canada and was "not too happy at the work rate" he found when he returned. "We are making slow but steady progress but I hesitate to make a firm date for sailing to America. I am still looking at leaving in the back end of April but it is very much touch and go. I just don't want to give you any bum information." To be safe, we turned down the alumni trip.

Two weeks later, Helen Ryle posted new information from the Project office. "All the major jobs are now finished on the ship but a myriad of small ones remain to be completed," she reported. "They expect to commence sea trials toward the end of April or early in May, and to depart for the US late in May for arrival there prior to the 4th of July."

I immediately contacted Mike Forwood. "The ship will not be sailing to America until mid-May at the earliest," he replied, "so go ahead and have your holiday." But by then it was too late; the Italian tour was fully booked.

At this juncture, as though a benign Providence recognized that my spirits needed a lift, a new email pen pal was about to come into my life. Chief Engineer Michael O'Carroll was the go-between: "I am passing on the email address of Deborah Steinbar, one of the people who has booked to sail on the maiden voyage," he wrote. 'She and her husband are Americans and wished to contact you."

Mike Forwood had mentioned a couple from New York who were signed-on crew members, and I immediately assumed these were the people. But no, they lived in Bemidji, Minnesota, "the one-and-only true home of Paul Bunyan and Babe the Blue Ox," as Deborah quickly reminded me.

Her husband Bill was a practicing family physician and amateur photographer; and she, after 20 years as a physician's assistant and nurse practitioner, was into a second career as a piano teacher and massage therapist. She was also a song writer and a member of an all-women's group that performed Celtic music. I pictured us sitting around in the ship's 'tween decks after the evening meal with Bill ministering to our bruises and seasickness while Deborah massaged our sore muscles and then entertained us with Irish folk songs.

I told Deborah about my grandmother, and she responded that both of her great- great grandmothers on her mother's side had sailed from Ireland during the famine (A quick calculation of generational spreads put Deborah's age at about 50, which she later corroborated).

"Their stories," she said, "and their history of having braved the sea are what I rely on for courage when I reflect on how difficult this voyage will be. I have great confidence that we will prevail, though we can't know how our gifts will be called upon until we are underway together. I think this will be the history-making trip of a lifetime and feel so fortunate to be able to make the commitment. Whoever we are today, we will certainly not be the same after the voyage."

We soon realized that just as we were inspired by a common dream and buoyed by a common hope, we were also adrift in the same confused seas.

The lack of a firm sailing date was playing even more havoc with Deborah and Bill's lives than it was with mine. Bill was required to take an every-six-years board reexamination. This was the year, and he needed to report for the exam on July 13 without fail. The latest guess was that we would leave Ireland in time to arrive in the US by July 4, but the date kept slipping week by week. "Depending on when and where we are," said Deborah, "Bill may have to abandon ship and fly back from somewhere."

"We've been through a lot together," I told her, "even before the ship sails. I don't know how many times I've played the voyage over in my mind as I expected it to unfold, only to have to put those thoughts away on the shelf for another month or two. There is now a dreamlike quality about the whole project, and if I hadn't actually been to Ireland and seen the ship it might seem like nothing but a shade, flitting in and out of consciousness like the Flying Dutchman."

Deborah was feeling much the same sense of unreality. "We've been through so many false starts," she said, "that it won't seem real when it actually happens." Like me, she had packed and repacked and didn't know anymore what was where.

Disparate news reports now began to pop up, causing our spirits to slump or soar, depending on where they stood on the *Jeanie Johnston* "reality" scale. In Philadelphia, where a Famine Memorial was being prepared on the waterfront in anticipation of the ship's visit, a major fund-raising event spawned a roster of speakers praising the *Jeanie Johnston* Project and the upcoming visit. Awards were handed out, pledges made and not a negative emotion appeared among all the smiling faces.

A few days later, Deborah emailed me: "Did you see the *Irish Examiner* online for March 22?" I looked and almost wished I hadn't.

"Famine Ship Project Under Threat as Budget Overruns by £5.5m," said the headline. It had appeared on March 22, within days of the big Philadelphia gathering. So the budget overrun was now up from £2 million to £5.5 million, fulfilling the prediction Helen Ryle had reported, and the money was still running out. The Irish Government had released more of the funds it had pledged to the Project but was still short by £900,000. Getting the rest of that money was urgent, said the *Jeanie Johnston* management, if the Project was to be completed and the ship sailed to America.

An article in one of the local Kerry newspapers put the situation in an even worse light. Unless the delayed Government funding came through, it said, "the troubled famine ship project could again be set back by several months." It went on to quote a Project executive as saying that if the funds were released, sea trials could be held at the end of April and the ship "will then be ready for its maiden voyage to the US later this year."

Those last three words settled on my spirits like a black cloud. "I was still coasting along merrily with an 'end-of-May' date fixed in mind," I told Deborah. "Now I don't know what to think." Already steeped in gloom, I sank deeper when Helen Ryle's message arrived with an editorial from another Kerry newspaper. This one didn't even try to be polite, calling the Project "a financial disaster."

The ship should have been built as a simple replica to sit at the Blennerville Pier, said the writer, not as a vessel equipped and qualified to sail the Atlantic. No real sailor could agree with that viewpoint, which was totally at odds with the vision that brought the *Jeanie Johnston* into being, though it was easy to see how critics could construe the Project as a case of over-reaching.

This new avalanche of bad news seemed to have convinced Deborah and Bill that it was time to pull out. "Bill is fed up with the situation," she wrote, "and is no longer interested in participating. Perhaps it just wasn't meant to be, and the 'real' voyage for us may have been the anticipation and dreams of the past year." She concluded with a bit of Celtic mysticism: "What great learning can come out of these 'dark' situations!"

I wasn't ready to give up the ship, though a crumb or two of reassuring information would surely help. Turlough McConnell was closer to the situation than anyone else this side of the Atlantic, and I could trust his advice. "It sounds to me as though the Jeanie is going down the drain, Turlough," I wrote. "Does the Irish/American community have enough pull to save it?"

"They would be hard pressed to raise the necessary funds," he responded, "without first being assured of a committed program of completion. After all the missed deadlines, coupled with a slow US economy, there will be few believers lined up to give money."

"No sailing date has been fixed," I said. "How realistic is a sailing this summer, assuming the ship is finished and the money is forthcoming? I'm trying to plan the next several months of my life, and I don't know how to do it."

The answer was dark indeed: "Tom, I suggest that you do not tie your plans around the *Jeanie Johnston* this summer. I'm no longer working for the project, though I'm available to help if the ship ever gets here. But by the sound of things from Tralee that is still doubtful, even for the year ahead."

I had asked for Turlough's honest advice. Now I had it.

But the roller coaster ride wasn't over. Two days later, messages arrived simultaneously from John Griffin and Michael O'Carroll. "Mike Forwood is away on leave," said Michael, "so I thought I should tell you the good news. The Irish Government has released the balance of the money promised to complete the ship. I suppose this now eliminates every known obstacle to completion, making it certain that we will sail for USA this summer."

John Griffin was even more specific: "The Irish Government has announced the final funding package to allow us to complete the Jeanie Johnston and sail to America in June. We expect work on the ship to be completed in April, with tests and sea trials in May. I'll keep you informed, and Mike will be in touch regarding the sea trials."

I had not expected to be aboard for the sea trials, though it now appeared that I might be. That possibility was quickly reversed, however, when I asked Michael to clarify. "I expect every berth will be required for "makers-men" and others who will not be able to sail the Atlantic," he wrote. I understood completely, and quickly said so.

Even so, all the pieces seemed to be going together-- once again. Helen Ryle noted that the foot-and-mouth disease that had been plaguing Irish dairymen was putting a crimp in the tourist season, with American tourists especially canceling their holidays, and the Irish Government and Tourist Board were trying to think of ways to woo the tourists back. "The *Jeanie Johnston* voyage, with the high-profile publicity it's sure to generate, should do a lot to restore confidence," she pointed out. "Just what the country needs right now."

Helen's web site reported that on May 4 "the Department of Marine is aiming for the Jeanie to go 'live' this weekend (May 5&6) and fire up the electrics and engines before she heads off on sea trials. She will then travel back to Cork and Cobh for a hull inspection. . .Sea trials and testing are expected to take about 10 days. . .Once she has been tested and certified, Jeanie can then set off on her long-awaited transatlantic voyage."

Helen further reported that a spokesman for the Project had announced on local radio that the ship would be finished within four weeks, sail to Cobh for hull inspection and then depart for America in June for a July landfall. This prediction never saw light as an official announcement, and I still had no official sailing date or date to report for crew training. But with a virtual tidal wave of unofficial information now rolling out of Tralee, I was desperate to make some plans.

"I need to have some plan in hand," I wrote Mike Forwood, "so I am making an airline reservation for May 27. You intimated the ship would be finished by May 5, so I'm assuming you'll get the sea trials done and go over to Cobh either before, or no later than, the week of May 20 and be back in Fenit the week of May 27. If I'm off by a week or more, please let me know."

"If you come over on May 27, that will be about right," Mike replied. "Our current plan is to sail on June 5, destination Quebec via the Azores, arriving July 4."

Here, suddenly, was a stunning piece of new information, out of thin air. So Quebec was back in the running! Not surprising, though. A crossing at this time of year could be made in the northern latitudes, and most likely that meant landfall somewhere between New York and Quebec. Another advantage of

105

this route: we were again closing in on the hurricane season, and a direct crossing would reduce our time at sea and thus reduce the likelihood of encountering a hurricane. An uneasy thought crossed my mind: hurricanes had been part of the rationale for canceling the voyage the previous July. But I consoled myself with the thought that weather hadn't been the only reason and may indeed have been somewhat of a scapegoat.

I made my plane reservation and quickly discovered that I was the unwitting member of yet another exclusive club. I had learned earlier that being over 75 made me persona non grata to the auto rental agencies. Now I found that anyone stupid enough to request a one-way ticket was penalized by being charged considerably more than the cost of a round trip. If there was any logic in that policy, I somehow failed to grasp it.

In the midst of this period of hope and uncertainty my 80th birthday rolled around. I had been 77 when the *Jeanie Johnston* first caught my attention, and 78 when I was accepted for a crew position. At 80, was I still a viable candidate for the voyage? or was I a crazy old man pursuing a feckless dream?

Was it time to let go of this obsession and live a normal life? The problem with that was that I wasn't attracted by the life style of most octogenarians. Some I knew had suffered a mental and emotional change at 80, as though that milepost was an automatic signal to feel old. The lives of others were dominated by physical infirmities. But I refused to believe our lives are controlled by numbers, and physically I was still holding my own.

I concluded, therefore, that I owed it to myself to continue pursuing my dream, though I had to admit that each passing year reduced physical stamina and mental concentration by a fraction. "Let's hope the *Jeanie Johnston* sails before I'm 90," I told Marie.

Nancy drove up from Maryland with the two little girls to help us celebrate. Nancy's gift was contained in a cardboard box that Caroline and Diana had decorated with crayon art. On its front was a seascape, with *Second Wind* bouncing over the waves and dolphins joyously leaping. Printed boldly across the sails was "Happy Birthday To You, Tom." The numerals "8" and "0" flashed across the sky in a motley array of bright colors, and a blazing yellow sun had "80" painted on its face. the boat's transom proclaimed its name, "80th *Second Wind*. On the side of the box, Caroline, a mathematician at nine, had written "80 is everything. It is 40x2 and 10x8. See?"

I wasn't sure that "80 is everything," but it certainly is a lot.

Within days of the birthday, a message arrived from Sue Tylor, the *Jeanie Johnston*'s cook. Mike Forwood was on leave, and Sue, acting on his behalf, was advising me that "plans to sail have been put back a further three weeks. This is necessary in order to complete the electrical work to the Department of Marine's satisfaction."

We had all been working tentatively with a June 15 sailing date (I had already changed my airline reservation twice), and it now looked as though the earliest date might be July 7 or 8. I e-mailed Deborah, though she had already heard from Michael O'Carroll, who added these details: "The completion has yet again been delayed-- but 3 to 4 weeks this time. The electrical contractor, who is the biggest source of delay, would not consider longer working days or a 24-hour shift pattern."

I caught John Griffin on the phone on June 21 and asked if sea trials were yet under way, as they should have been. No, he said, they've been held up by those persistent electrical problems. Deborah, meanwhile, came up with the following intelligence: "They're going ahead with purchasing things, i.e. cookery, etc., but there are definitely two opposing points of view-- one that wants her to be totally readied before departure and one that says 'we've got to get to America or the whole project is doomed.'"

There was more to the electrical problem than Deborah or I then realized. We both incorrectly assumed that little, inconsequential finishing-up chores were now getting in the way of sailing and that the forces of perfection were arrayed against the forces of action.

I emailed John Griffin: "There have been so many postponements, changes and uncertainties that even many in the Irish/American community have no faith any more in the ship or the aims of the project, and those of the general public who know about it have written off the whole idea as the bemused dream of a group of befuddled Irishmen.

"There now seem to be two factions at work in the decision-making process-- those devoted to getting the ship to a state of utter perfection with no regard for her purpose, and those who understand that she can redeem herself only by sailing to America as soon as possible. If Jeanie does not sail this summer, she risks becoming the laughingstock of the Western World."

John responded graciously to my harsh message: "I fully appreciate your concerns. You have always had the Project's interests at heart. The bottom line is that the *Jeanie Johnston* is very near completion. All systems are operational, and she will be ready for sea trials next weekend. The Senior Surveyor of the Irish Department of Marine is due to visit the ship tomorrow and hopefully we will have a positive outcome. The Department has the final say whether or not the ship will sail to North America this year.

"I hope you will keep the faith," he concluded. "Once the ship sails out of Tralee Bay, I believe much of the skepticism will evaporate and confidence will return."

It had become my habit to access my email every morning before breakfast. Eight am on the US east coast was 1 pm in Ireland, so any morning mail from Tralee would be waiting for me. Two days after John Griffin's response, I had two messages, one from Helen Ryle and the other from Michael O'Carroll. I read them in a state of shock:

Subject: End of the dream
Dear Tom:
Sorry to be the bearer of bad news, but I just now heard on

108

*the National Radio News that the Jeanie Johnston Project
has been "abandoned." A very short piece; it just said that
the Department of Marine had announced the abandonment
"with regret."
I don't know if the whole project is abandoned or if they will
find some use for Jeanie, but I guess it means the end of the
US voyage. Such a shame, after all that work, money,
people's time, financial and emotional involvement.
Yours in sorrow for the end of a beautiful dream.
Helen*

*Subject: Bad News
Regretfully, I must advise that the Atlantic trip has been can-
celled. News was broadcast on local radio this afternoon
after a board meeting. Following a visit by the Department
of Marine inspector who was unhappy with the quantity
and quality of electrical work done, some decisions were
made in Dublin. Can only speculate after that.
Regards
Michael O'C*

I sat for a while with my head in my hands and then began to
wonder vaguely what I would do next.

CHAPTER 9

The Ship is Under Arrest

Waiting for the *Jeanie Johnston* was like spending my life on amusement park rides.

First, the roller coaster. Emotionally, I was either up, down or on my way to one or the other.

Then there was the merry-go-round. Whatever happened last year, the seasons would make their circuit and bring me back to the same point this year. Washington, New York, Savannah and Quebec-- all had enjoyed brief prominence as the landfall city, only to fade away and return, one after another, a year later.

Since that July day on the Irish naval ship Eithne almost a year before, I had made a complete circuit. The message then-- and now-- was a sudden and unexpected "Voyage called off!"

"I'm walking around in a daze," Deborah wrote. "My focus for the past two years has been on the JJ, so I'm a little lost right now. Trying to refocus my energies and creativity into other interests, and trying to process this 'journey.'"

At first I, too, thought the ride was over for good, but now clues to a softer fate were beginning to emerge.

The radio broadcast Helen Ryle had heard did indeed use the word "abandoned:" "The decision to abandon the sailing," it said, "was made after a maritime expert reported that technical systems, crew training and other fit-outs could not be completed in time to safely make an Atlantic crossing this year."

But in the *Irish Times*, the word was "canceled," and Frank Fahey, Minister for the Marine, expressed "disappointment and regret," but said he was committed to completing the Project. And the *Irish Independent* reported that the Project's organizers "promised the Atlantic crossing will take place in 2002."

I had just written Michael O'Carroll ("What a rotten ending to such a noble idea! I wish I were there to go off to the pub with you and get drunk") and had thanked Helen for her timely if unwelcome news and told her I wasn't sure what I'd do next when John Griffin called to say that the reports of the Jeanie's death were greatly exaggerated. "With work running late," he said, "the prudent decision was to postpone the voyage to next year. The Minister for the Marine has said that the ship will go to North America next year. In the meantime it will undergo sea trials and sail around Ireland."

There was the carrot dangling before me again. And suddenly there was more.

"The ship will be doing a mid-August cruise around Ireland," said John. "Dublin, Belfast, Cork. How would you like to be aboard?"

Here was the merry-go-round again, I thought. The same voyage in Irish waters I'd been offered the year before. But I thanked John and said I'd love to be aboard.

My life had become a constant process of sorting out. Every time a new set of circumstances came over the horizon, it was time to analyze the situation anew. I knew-- or thought I knew-- where we were yesterday. But where were we today? I asked Helen Ryle and Michael O'Carroll what they thought.

Helen was taking it philosophically. "You'd be surprised to hear in the radio interviews how much support there still is for the Project from both David Ervine in the north and Minister Fahey down here. There will be an uproar locally about the money spent, and I think things will churn a lot in the next week, with plenty of recriminations flying. Then, if things go as intended, and Jeanie goes on sea trials in August, the Project may return to a more even keel. I hope you won't jump ship!"

"The ship is 'on the edge' of being ready for sea," Michael O'Carroll told me. If a little more of the wiring had been completed, said Michael, she could have been taken out on sea trials. But now the experience of the electrical contractor and the quality of his work were being questioned. Some work already done would have to be redone.

"Work on the ship is continuing," Michael wrote, "even as I type." I could picture him in the large bright room on the second floor of the Lifesaving Station that was the *Jeanie Johnston*'s operations office at the Fenit pier. "It is Saturday a.m. here and the lads are in on overtime."

I had told Michael I wanted to restore some order to my life, not just live from broken date to broken date. "You and Mike must feel bad," I'd said, "for having given us those dates in good faith only to see them broken, one after another."

"We were let down by a contractor," he replied. "But Rome was not built in a day. When you look at comparative building times for ships like this one, this one holds up to scrutiny. And the hand-over of a completed ship is often fraught with complications-- like a difficult delivery."

"The *Jeanie Johnston*," he added, warming to his subject, "will be delivered by Caesarian Section!"

Michael, Mike Forwood, the O'Regan brothers, John Griffin -- they had all put much more time into the project than anyone ever anticipated. They still believed in the ship and they needed ongoing support from me and anyone else who was in a position to give it.

What Michael told me next-- whether he intended this result or not-- virtually ensured that I would not desert the project.

"The house flag," he said," is being drawn up by the Herald at the Genealogical Office. It is to be a dove against a blue background with a few white waves, emphasizing the 'Ship of Peace' aspect of the project. After America, I could see us going to Australia, South Africa and eventually sailing to the eastern Mediterranean with a mixed crew of Arabs and Jews, then doing the same with people from other conflict-torn areas."

I remembered the Irish teen-agers, Catholic and Protestant, who had worked together on the framing and planking of the ship and had gone home with attitudes forever changed. This was a vision of more grandeur than anything I had read or heard among the thousands of words written about the ship, and I resolved to keep it close to my heart in the event I ever faltered.

Meanwhile, the Irish press was clobbering the *Jeanie Johnston* Project unmercifully. "The sad saga of Jeanie". . ."A tale of a shipwreck". . ."The Project was shipwrecked before the ship entered the water". . ."*Jeanie Johnston*. . .tourism flagship or millstone around Kerry's neck?". . ."*Jeanie Johnston* plagued by difficulties."

There's an old comedy line: "They said 'Cheer up, things could be worse.' So I cheered up, and sure enough, things got worse." In the midst of the flying brickbats, when I thought things couldn't get worse, Helen Ryle told me they could.

The project had barely bounced back from the setback of the abandoned voyage when it was plunged into a new controversy.

After the Department of Marine inspector failed to certify the ship's electrical system, a dispute broke out between the Project management and the electrical contractor. The company said it had paid the contractor £87,000 for work that proved to be defective and "not in accordance with required standards." The contractor, in turn, said he was owed more than £100,000 and had been given "a very vague specification" for the job. He refused to leave the ship and kept a skeleton crew on board, effectively preventing another electrician from coming aboard and proceeding with the work.

Most alarming of all, the contractor threatened to call in a receiver and put the ship into liquidation to recover the money owed to him. "Ending up with a receiver," a local newspaper reported, "would likely sink the Jeanie for good."

113

"The whole sorry mess goes to the Circuit Court here in Tralee next week," Helen told me. "The only good news is that the ship is 99 per cent finished, and the electrical work is all that's left to do."

But as a result of the failed inspection, newspapers were now reporting that the ship had been found "not seaworthy," and rumors to that effect spread so quickly that in no time at all Paddy Powers, a major bookmaker in Dublin, was offering 20 to one odds that she would sink during her sea trials.

While the lawyers sparred, the ship was opened to the public for the first time in early July, and the initial weekend was a surprising success. Some 3,000 visitors from as far away as the US, Spain, Germany, Denmark, England and Belarus admired the impressive rigging, the fine craftsmanship, the lovingly polished wood and John Griffin's theatrical magic at work in the 19th century 'tween decks museum.

One visitor, a former shipyard worker and merchant seaman from Belfast, urged Americans and Canadians to bear with the project and be sure to visit the ship when she arrives in America. "She is part of your history," he said, "and you will not be disappointed."

He had less positive words about the planning and construction: "I have stood by several ships under construction at some of the world's leading shipyards, and it quickly came across to me that however small the vessel and however enthusiastic the constructors, it was never going to happen in the time frame given. In this case the choice of Fenit as a fitting out and completion harbor was totally flawed. I shudder to think of the logistics/cost of getting specialized components and materials in such a place."

Deborah by now had recovered a good measure of her customary insouciance, though the likelihood of their doing the voyage seemed to be fading for her and Bill, largely because of Bill's inflexible work schedule and the total impossibility-- as we both had learned-- of making any kind of plan tied to the

Jeanie Johnston's timing. They decided early in July to forsake the dream and ask that their voyage fee be returned. "I certainly hope we get a chance to meet some day," she said in a message that sounded for all the world like a farewell letter.

"Your last email sounded as though we may be forever lost to one another," I quipped. "No, not lost forever," she replied. "We'd like to sail on the round-Ireland tour, but we're afraid we may not be invited now that we've given up the Atlantic voyage. Besides, we're tired of trying to live in the next 'couple of months' without being able to trust in much that we hear."

As it turned out, they needn't have worried about the round-Ireland tour. We didn't know then, though we soon began to suspect, that even this mini-voyage was in trouble, as it had been a year earlier. The company and the dethroned electrical contractor had agreed on a neutral surveyor who would go aboard and assess the nature and quality of the electrical work, but there was a possible downside to that action. "When a surveyor comes on the scene," said Michael O'Carroll, "every minor problem becomes a major one. That's how surveyors earn their money."

As day after day was spent reviewing the electrical specifications, the window of opportunity for the Irish tour grew smaller and smaller. At first, the plan had been to circumnavigate the island-country, stopping at every major port. Now Mike Forwood considered avoiding the west coast since the weather there gets nasty as fall approaches. Instead, he was proposing an Irish Sea tour, with stops at Waterford, Belfast and then over to Glasgow and Liverpool. An advantage of this plan was that it would broaden the ship's audience a bit before the ocean voyage by touching briefly at ports of two other countries.

But now that the Irish Department of the Marine was calling the shots, another bureaucratic monkey wrench was thrown into the works. Once the final plan for the revised electrical work was drawn up, it had to be submitted to the Department for review, and then, in the manner of government bureaus, it would be sent out for bids. That surely meant several more weeks before the wiring could even be started.

When I talked to Michael O'Connell toward the end of August, he sounded glum about the immediate future. "I expect we'll sail for the US early in January, with a little bit of coastal work before then," he said. "I suppose we'll have sea trials some time in November."

By this time, I had been communicating for months, sometimes almost daily, with Michael, Mike Forwood, John Griffin and Helen Ryle, but it took a sudden tragedy to make me realize how closely our lives had become intertwined.

Helen was on holiday in Spain on the infamous date of September 11, and three days after the terrorist attacks she sent this message from an internet cafe: "It was with absolute horror that we learned of the attacks on New York and the Pentagon on Tuesday. Our shop in Tralee is closed today as a mark of respect for your dead, as are all businesses, shops, bars, etc. in the whole of Ireland. I hope no one belonging to you was killed or injured in the attacks. I wanted to let you know that we are thinking of you and praying for you."

Mike Forwood, too, obviously on the run, telegraphed this terse message: "All devastated here by events in New York. You have our support. With regards to the JJ, the ship is effectively finished except for the electrical wiring. All things on hold basically, and many staff have gone. But still no reason why we cannot be in USA for 2002."

Following the September 11 attacks, the transatlantic voyage seemed to make even more sense-- and offer more value-- than it had. Mike seconded this thought, noting that "people here seem to be aware that recent events make the JJ trip to America even more important." In the wake of 9/11, American tourism in Ireland was expected to drop dramatically, and the arrival of the ship in America could only have a positive effect, sparking renewed interest in all things Irish and offsetting, at least to some extent, the fear of flying.

If so, why was nothing happening? The Department of Ma-

116

rine, which was now paying the bills for work on the ship, had convened a focus group in Dublin and directed its members to recommend ideas for the ship's future. That in itself sounded ominously uncertain, and the timetable-- the group was to report in January, 2002-- didn't offer much hope for speedy action.

"If the Jeanie Johnston would bolster tourism," I wrote Mike, "why aren't people moving faster? If they need a fire lighted under them, how about a letter-writing campaign from Irish/American officials in the US and others with a stake in the voyage? There must be someone with the authority to speed things up. The longer the work drags on, the less interest there is here in the US. As for myself, I have no way of scheduling anything in my life until I know what the voyage plans are. If you could let me know when the electrical work starts, that at least might give me some hope."

Mike's frustration was even greater than mine. "I've told them that if they want a full and proper season in the States next year, I must leave in mid-January and cross via the Canaries and Caribbean to arrive by St. Patrick's Day. But I've said that before and it hasn't happened. Despite what we'd hoped, the electrical work hasn't started yet. We are still waiting for the quotes to come back. Meanwhile, most of the labor force has gone, and the Government is fast losing interest."

Then, in the first crack I'd seen in his stoic sea-captain composure, he confided "All of this delay and indecision does nothing for my confidence in the Project. However, I'm hanging in at the moment."

A month later, Helen Ryle, under pressure to report something, could only say that "The *Jeanie Johnston* project managers currently await Department of Marine approval to undertake the completion of work on the ship, which would mean that sea trials could commence in early spring, 2002."

Early in November, I picked up some snippets of information from various people in Tralee. Michael O'Carroll was on paid leave and had taken a job on a survey ship operating out of Trin-

117

idad. Mike Forwood was back home in the UK and would not return until January. The Department of Marine was being "quite difficult," and outside accountants were scouring the records, demanding "real" figures.

"Not an awful lot of work" was being done on the ship. A company in Cork finally got the electrical contract and was scheduled to start work on November 19. It was expected to take eight weeks. Some time around January 10 the ship would go into dry dock in Cork, and sea trials would follow. The maiden voyage might take place in March or April, but everyone stressed that no decisions had yet been made.

In strict compliance with Murphy's law, the next piece of information-- early in December-- was worse than the previous one. At a meeting of the Department of Marine focus group in Dublin, Brendan Dinneen, now the Project's general manager, was reported by the newspaper *Kerry's Eye* as saying that the ship would sail but the voyage would not be the Company's responsibility.

"It is not the Jeanie Johnston Company which will be undertaking the voyage," he was quoted as saying. "Our task will be to complete work on the ship, undertake the necessary sea trials and get the ship to sea." He denied, in response to rumors, that the ship was for sale.

Now I had two unknowns to deal with: (1) When, if ever, was the ship going to sail? and (2) When and if she did sail, who would be her owner? Would I be required to apply anew for a crew berth? Must I go through again that whole protracted process of trying to demonstrate I was fit for an ocean voyage? And then the terrible thought took root: Two years after fighting my way past the age barrier, maybe I finally <u>was</u> too old.

I gave that possibility a passing thought and concluded that I could make that decision only when faced with the actuality of a sailing date. Meanwhile, I must simply hang in there and wait.

The year sputtered to a close amid reports that some crew members were asking for refunds of their voyage fees. I decided to leave mine where it was rather than risk having to start all over again. The money was in a special account at the *Jeanie Johnston* Project, where I was assured it was safe from whatever financial catastrophes might befall the company.

How many more New Year's Eves would there be, I wondered, before the voyage became a solid reality? Two years earlier, Marie and I had toasted my upcoming adventure, assumed to be only three or four months away in early 2000. As the year 2000 wound down, I had consumed myself in a rash outburst of misdirected energy, and fired off on New Year's Day a proposed voyage newsletter that no one responded to or knew what to do with. Now the year 2001 was coming to an end, and we were in the same void we'd been in for the past two years.

Fred Gates of the Coast Guard Auxiliary, now its National Public Affairs Officer, was still waiting for my daily voyage reports. Wondering, perhaps, if my hoped-for adventure might always have been no more than the fluff of an Irish mist, Fred asked me if I'd like to join his National Press Corps, a group of volunteer writers who report on Auxiliary activities.

I told Fred the ship "seemed poised for a spring voyage," and that I'd best not become engaged in any other activities. But how could I know?

We'd decided the only way to plan vacation trips was to put them as close to the end of the following year as possible, assuming the *Jeanie Johnston* would sail in the first half of the year. But we'd applied the same thinking the year before, and the year before that, and the ship never sailed. How would next year be any different?

Ominously, the year 2002 promised to be different in at least one way: the headlines from Ireland were bigger-- and blacker. The first headline of the year came early in February:

HIGH COURT PLACES JEANIE UNDER ARREST

The electrical contractor had invoked an obscure 18th century

119

Admiralty law that permitted a ship to be arrested for debt. His application to the High Court of Ireland had produced an arrest order, local authorities had posted the order on the ship, and the ship had been placed under security watch. The Jeanie Johnston Company promised not to move the ship out of jurisdiction. The ship, in other words, would not try to escape.

This was the stuff of Gilbert and Sullivan. I pictured the constable walking down the dock, arrest warrant in hand, confronting the ship and barking out, "*Jeanie Johnston*, by order of the High Court, I place you under arrest! Any attempt on your part to escape will have the most serious consequences." I wasn't sure what he could have done with a pair of handcuffs, but he might have chained and padlocked her to the dock.

One thing was now certain: as long as the ship was under arrest, she was not going anywhere-- to the US, to Cork, or even across the bay to the Dingle peninsula. Any potential voyage was strictly on hold.

Now, in addition to the electrical contractor, two other contractors were suing the Company for alleged nonpayment of outstanding bills. The problem seemed to center on the Blennerville shipyard, which the Company hoped to sell, using the proceeds to pay off its debts. The little shipyard was in an area of growing land values, and the potential buyer, the Aquadome, planned to build a major tourist attraction on the site. But there were liens against the property, and all the pieces hadn't yet fallen into place to permit the sale to be finalized.

"The saga continues," Mike Forwood wrote, "and we are now in a legal minefield."

The Project, which had gone more than four times over budget-- from 3.81 million euros to just under 16 million euros (On January 1, 2002, Ireland switched from pounds to euros)-- was now the target for creditors far and wide. Documents released under the Freedom of Information Act showed that a consultant's report by Ernst and Young had found serious problems as early as 1999. The report, said the *Irish Inde-*

pendent, "highlighted serious deficiencies in work schedules and warned that a failure to sail as planned in 2000 'would be catastrophic for the Project.'"

Marine Minister Frank Fahey was quoted in the *Independent* as saying the *Jeanie Johnston* Project "has been the big headache of my two years in this Department." While Mr. Fahey had been instrumental in getting additional millions for the ship, he now wasn't sure he should have done that.

But former Minister for Foreign Affairs Dick Spring, an early champion of the project, noted that "the *Jeanie Johnston* was a valuable asset, and the voyage to the United States was a fundamental part of the project." He went on to say that "there is a huge anticipation by the Irish community in the States, and that the ship still had valuable potential for marketing Ireland in America."

Of the thousands of words now being written about the Project, often the most trenchant and always the most colorful were those of Padraig Kennelly, a columnist for the weekly newspaper *Kerry's Eye*.

"On Wednesday," he wrote, "the *Jeanie Johnston* Project was as much on the rocks as the Spanish trawler *Celestial Dawn* at the mouth of Dingle Harbour." Much of her cost overrun, he noted, was due to "layers of consultants supervising other consultants." On the Jeanie's relationship to Blennerville, the village of her birth: "Part of the projected earnings of the *Jeanie Johnston* were to be as a visitor attraction at Blennerville. The boat had to be lifted from Blennerville to Fenit on a barge costing almost a quarter of a million pounds. If the Jeanie were to come back into Blennerville it would cost the same money again and she would be there until she rotted on the mud flats."

Ticking off a list of high Government officials and political leaders who had visited the ship and whose opinions were now being invoked, Kennelly observed that this "combined group of famous heads would not have the skill to assess the viability of a 12-foot rowing boat."

"When the Jeanie was launched at Fenit," he wrote, "it had a full crew paraded on the pier, yet the boat was unfit to go to the next parish. The *Jeanie Johnston* statements spawned more flowery Celtic phrases than you'll find in James Stephens' *The Crock of Gold* and William Butler Yeats' *The Wanderings of Oisin* put together, but that hot air did little to fill the sails."

In the midst of the newspapers' feeding frenzy, the long-awaited focus group report was finally released. There was little in it to offer much hope. The report spelled out three possible scenarios for the disposition of the *Jeanie Johnston*: (1) No further State support. When the ship was completed, she would be sold and the proceeds used to pay off her debts; (2) Enough State support to get her to America, but that's all. She would then stay in North America under some kind of plan not yet in existence or she would be sold there; (3) The Jeanie could become the property of the State and be used as a sail training or museum ship.

The fly in the ointment was that all three options involved State funding-- and the State was not inclined to invest another penny. The Marine Minister was quoted as saying that the Project should be wound down and the creditors paid.

What should be done with the *Jeanie Johnston*? Everyone seemed to have an idea, and, strangely enough, the American voyage was no longer among them. It was, said one spokesman, "currently on the back burner." A sail training ship appealed to some, a museum ship to others. And then a group of private investors came up with a dreadful plan that was actually presented to the Government: turn the Jeanie into a prison ship.

I thought of the ship, in all her quiet majesty, sitting there at the dock, her destiny still unfulfilled. How unfair it all was--to her, and to me.

CHAPTER 10

Headed For the Auctioneer's Block

Out of such pain and suffering there must come some kind of redemption.

That seemed to be Padraig Kennelly's view, and I desperately wanted to make it mine. "The events of the past week have drifted the *Jeanie Johnston* into the eye of a financial and political storm," he wrote. "They have also spawned the third media obituary of a sailing ship that has yet to get its first push forward by the winds. The pain suffered in the project will make the Jeanie a very desirable visitor to American ports. They will be quite interested in visiting a ship that rose from the dead three times before her sails were unfurled."

Kennelly urged that the final lien on the shipyard property be lifted, the property sold and debts paid off, and that the American voyage be funded by the Tourist Boards of Ireland and Northern Ireland "to help both regions recover from the effects of foot and mouth disease and the September 11 damage to tourism on this island."

But the "Jeanie Affair" was now a hot potato being tossed from hand to hand by the Government, the Kerry County Council and the Tralee Town Council. All had invested substantial sums of money in the project, and there was concern that the

Government was about to wash its hands of the matter, leaving the County and the taxpayers of Tralee to hold the bag.

There was much finger-pointing, charges of dereliction of duty, accusations that those who should have been watchful were asleep at the switch. "The dogs in the street have known the Project has been in trouble for a number of years," said the county's other weekly paper, *The Kerryman*, "yet it took almost two full years for the hammer to fall."

Little good news was to be found in those dreary February days, but a small glimmer of light came through when Helen Ryle emailed the news that the arrest order had been lifted by the High Court. That would permit work on the ship to continue. She had heard, too, that the Jeanie Johnston Company was to be "wound down in a structured manner."

And the storm of media comment had included a Kerry Radio interview with Bob Gessler, President of the Philadelphia branch of the Ancient Order of Hibernians, who was, said Helen, "really upbeat, saying it didn't matter how long it took to get Jeanie to the US, that there is real grassroots support for the voyage, and that they plan to have a month-long Irish festival centered around her arrival."

John Griffin wrote me a reassuring note, too, saying "There is little consideration at this time of the Irish/American dimension or appreciation of the potential of the ship's visit to the US. Those of us who have visited America know the impact will be substantial and rewarding."

I was curious to know how the situation looked from the Captain's viewpoint. Mike Forwood was back from England now, and I caught up with him early in March.

"Everything imaginable has happened to this ship," he said. "I don't know what more could happen to it." Mike was virtually alone now. Michael O'Carroll was still there, but only on a volunteer basis, and no other permanent crew members were left. The electrical work was underway, and he thought sea trials might be conducted around Easter time.

"We definitely won't be able to go to America this year," Mike said. "I'd like to do a midsummer cruise around Ireland -- something on a lower key, to gradually build back some confidence in the ship."

I can't say I was surprised. But strangely enough, I was not greatly distressed by this news. My priorities, I realized, had shifted. For two years, my total concern had been to sail as soon as possible as a crew member on the North American voyage. Now the most important thing was to save the ship. There would be no triumphant maiden voyage if the *Jeanie Johnston* were turned into a prison ship, or if she were sold for debt to some unknown person or organization. Saving the ship came first. After that, I could worry about the voyage.

But even Mike's modest summer plan might run into roadblocks. The County and Town Councils were moving to take over the ship in the short term, he said, and there was a strong desire on the part of some to keep the ship at Fenit, or at most sail it to nearby Dingle during the 2002 tourist season, gathering support and raising funds for the US voyage. "It will take a new group, with new thinking, to get the ship to America any sooner," he added.

I wanted to know what it meant for the project to be "wound down in a structured manner," and Helen Ryle tried to enlighten me. "There have been a lot of conflicting reports," Helen said, but here's how she saw the situation developing:

When the Kerry and Tralee Councils took over responsibility for the project, they would continue to support the ship's completion and sea trials. But they were sticking their necks out by agreeing to put up the additional money needed. Unless this and the other millions they'd already pledged could be recouped through income from the ship's voyages, the taxpayers would foot the bill for years to come. When the shipyard was sold, the proceeds should pay all the creditors and see enough left for the sea trials.

The Councils had supported the Project from the start. They

didn't want to see the Jeanie sold off cheaply, which is what would happen if the creditors called in a liquidator. They did want to keep the ship in Kerry as a visitor attraction if the Atlantic voyage couldn't be arranged. They were fully aware that they could only attain their highest monetary return if the ship went on a successful US voyage, but at the moment they didn't see where the money would come from to make that possible.

"The overall impression I get," said Helen, "is that everybody is expecting something to happen to save the day-- maybe some little bit of Irish magic."

The magic was slow in coming, but things were at least beginning to move in the right direction. The Irish press reported in mid-March that work on the Jeanie should be completed by the end of the month, sea trials would be conducted in Tralee Bay, and the ship would then go into dry dock in Cobh to have her hull examined. The court case involving the electrical contractor was adjourned for a month, and meetings on the plan for Kerry and Tralee to take over the ship were progressing, but slowly.

In late March I had a talk with Brendan Dinneen, who had replaced John Griffin as project director, and Brendan was able to fill in some of the information chinks and give me a more complete picture of what was happening. "There's been a lot of legal prancing at high levels," he said, "but the consensus among all parties is that the ship is a real asset and it would be a shame to send it to Monrovia just to pay off the debts."

The Jeanie Johnston Company would take the ship through its sea trials, and the ship would then become the property of the Kerry Council, which would take over the company's assets and liabilities. The Council would ensure that creditors were paid, then operate the ship as a tourist attraction for the balance of 2002, "giving everyone a chance to stop and take a breath; then, without pressure, think through what happens next."

The likely schedule, said Brendan, was that the ship would be open to tourists from May to July and would then go sailing round Ireland in August, September and October.

126

Michael O'Boyle, he told me, had left the Project several months earlier but the O'Regans were still with it. Mike Forwood's future depended on what happened. If the ship sailed, she'd need a captain; if she didn't, she wouldn't.

I heard for the first time the bloody details of the condemned electrical installation: "If you saw some of the electrical work," he said, "you would weep. Every cable, every junction box, had to be torn out and replaced. They'd used the wrong cable, mixed different cables, had different kinds of cables coming into the same junction box, etc. The deckhouses had to be removed, all the interior paneling had to be taken off to get at the wiring, the whole system had to be replaced."

The big job, said Brendan, was to restore credibility. "Some people think the ship is not seaworthy. We have to convince them it is."

A few days later, on April 6, Michael O'Carroll dispatched to the full "Friends of the *Jeanie Johnston*" list what had to be the first official communication from the ship itself: "Just a brief note to advise progress on the ship. Dock trials were completed alongside on Thursday with engines and generators running under load. Yesterday we completed the initial sea trials during a five-hour trip into Tralee Bay. Engines and steering, anchors and windlass, compass and radio gear were all successfully put through their paces. The ship is scheduled to travel to Cork on Tuesday for a brief dry dock period. No sails have been set yet as the rigging must be finally adjusted."

It was a straightforward message, but I detected in its tone, and in the fact that it was sent at all, a quietly triumphant "I told you so" to those whose faith might have been faltering.

Helen Ryle reported additional details: that the ship "was being tested to very exacting standards as a Class 7 cargo vessel able to carry passengers-- a much higher specification than that of a sailing ship." Mike Forwood said he was delighted with the way the ship handled and that she was "steady as a rock."

At the same time the *Jeanie Johnston* was throwing out her

127

first bow wave, the first Irish summer tourist season since 9/11 was about to begin, and the predictions were gloomy indeed. "Some industry experts are predicting a drop of one third or more in the number of American tourists in the aftermath of the September 11 attacks," *The Kerryman* reported. "Alarm bells are ringing in the tourism industry," said the *Irish Independent*. "All signals are worrying in the wake of September 11, with industry chiefs reporting a dramatic 40 to 60 percent fall in coach tour traffic-- the mainstay of many seasonal hotels."

Four top Irish tourism industry executives were mentioned in the several articles, and the strategies they were proposing-- cutting costs, more government funding, more value-for-money packages, aggressively marketing abroad in high-yield areas-- seemed all rather generalized and missing a specific opportunity that was right before their noses.

I wrote to all four, suggesting that there might be a more subtle factor contributing to the tourist slump-- the failure of the *Jeanie Johnston* to fulfill the expectations of thousands of Irish/Americans up and down the US East Coast.

"Two years ago," I wrote, "members of the Irish/American community were stirred to fever pitch by the *Jeanie Johnston* Project, and elaborate plans were developed for art exhibits, folk festivals and cultural pageants to welcome the ship to each of her ports of call. As plans were canceled again and again, much of the good feeling about Ireland was dissipated, giving way to negative rumblings. For many, Ireland has lost its luster and for some it has become a joke.

"The Irish tourist industry has, in the *Jeanie Johnston*, the single most potent tool it could find for giving the tourist business a jump start. The ship at present is a wasted resource that could be doing a major service for the Irish nation. Get her launched on her Atlantic voyage. When she arrives triumphantly in American port cities, all grievances will be forgotten, the Irish spirit will be restored, and Irish/Americans will begin to think once more with pleasure and nostalgia about the old country."

What impact the letter had, I don't know. I never heard from any of the tourist executives, though the yachting magazine *Ireland Afloat* did reprint the letter in a special comment section about the future of the *Jeanie Johnston*.

Helen Ryle and I now began trading ideas about how to make the US voyage happen. Helen had some computer-savvy thoughts, like a private chat room where everybody interested could get useful real-time exchanges of ideas going, and a circulated mailing list, where everybody receives a copy of all mail sent by everybody else. Helen was on to a seminal idea-- to get interested people, volunteers and supporters in the US together to help plan the voyage-- but would anyone listen?

On April 9, the Jeanie embarked on what might be called her maiden voyage, though I preferred to reserve that term for her American venture. Helen's spirited description on her web site couldn't be bettered:

"Tuesday 9th April saw the *Jeanie Johnston* head out to the open ocean for her maiden voyage to Cork. I joined an enthusiastic group of onlookers at the dockside and watched as the Captain and crew made their final preparations, including a safety briefing for all hands.

"Buses had brought local school children to witness this historic event, and everyone was in great form, chatting to the people nearest them and cheering and clapping as the chequered green and gold Kerry flag was hoisted to the mast top.

"At just after 1 pm the crew took in the gangplank and cast off the bow lines. Jeanie slowly turned towards the harbour exit, and her diesel engines could be felt vibrating the dockside with their power. Then the stern lines were cast off, and the ship needed no tug to help her to the pier's end as she headed majestically for open water.

"Everybody on the dockside waved and shouted their good wishes, and Captain Forwood and his crew waved back at us. Jeanie turned round the end of Fenit Pier and headed toward open water and the Atlantic Ocean, unfurling her mainsails as she went. Her voyage to Cork will take 24 hours, conducting further tests along the way, and she is expected to return to Fenit in about two weeks' time."

The following morning, Radio Kerry interviewed Mike Forwood live on a ship-to-shore line. All systems had worked perfectly, he said. They were then rounding the Old Head of Kinsale, and he expected an escort of tugs and local launches to welcome them into Cork

The ship arrived in Cork just in time to help commemorate the 100th anniversary of the *Titanic*'s departure from nearby Cobh on her maiden voyage, and her first official duty was to join the Irish national sail training ship *Asgard II* and the Irish naval ship *Eithne,* which we had visited in New York almost two years earlier, to lay a commemorative wreath offshore.

If there was any doubt about public interest in the *Jeanie Johnston*, it was soon dispelled. During the days she was open to visitors at the Cork dock and at the Heritage Centre in Cobh, as many as 900 a day came aboard, and all were impressed by what they saw. The Lord Mayor of Cork welcomed the ship with a Civic Reception attended by Government, community and business leaders, and there was a good deal of interest in chartering the ship for corporate functions over the coming months.

Suddenly, everything was coming up roses. The ship had passed the most rigorous tests of her systems and her sailing abilities, both at sea and in dry dock, and was now approved by the Department of Marine, her former nemesis. She had met all international requirements and was certified to sail anywhere in the world. The public loved her. And a number of crew members had had the good luck to be on her first (if not "maiden") voyage. I envied them a bit, though I understood that they were local supporters to whom the invitation had been extended, and they had paid for the privilege of crewing, as I would.

But I was still a long way from having that personal experience, and the passage of time didn't ease the problem. Since 1998, when I had first seen the embryonic ship in Blennerville, four years had passed. It was May again, and May brought another birthday. Like it or not, I was 81.

I'd read of a coast-hopping tall ship in Australia from which a crew member had opted out before the completion of the cruise because, in his own words, "It's just too much. After all, I have a 54-year-old body." Was Captain Mike Forwood having doubts about my 81-year-old body? If the ship ever sailed to America, would he want me aboard? What could I do to demonstrate that I was still alive and able-bodied?

Fortunately, the Coast Guard Auxiliary came up with a timely answer. It was offering a five-day Boat Crew School at the Coast Guard Training Center in Cape May, New Jersey. If I could complete that school with a passing grade, my reward would be a certificate stating that I was qualified to serve as a crew member on Coast Guard patrols. That piece of paper could be an insurance policy for me in Ireland.

Age is no major issue in the Auxiliary. Many Auxiliarists join in retirement and do useful work standing watch in Coast Guard stations, instructing in safe boating courses and conducting safety examinations of pleasure craft. To be sure, though, I contacted a friend who was an instructor in the school and he personally signed me up.

It wasn't easy. My classmates and I wore the Coast Guard's dark blue work uniforms, stood 0530 reveille and attended classes and demonstrations from 0700 to 2230. We were required to don immersion suits, jump in and swim across a pool. On the bay, we practiced man overboard drills, towing disabled boats, navigating in the dark and much more.

No one talked about age, and I was determined that, from my perspective, they would not have cause to do so. Our classroom building was about a mile from the barracks, and the majority of my fellow students--in their 40s, 50s and 60s, mostly-- drove to class. I walked. I needed the exercise and I wanted to demonstrate that I was reasonably fit. It seemed to work.

Later, there was an all-day grilling by Coast Guard Qualification Examiners, and eventually, the certificates were handed out. Mine went into my long-ago-packed duffle bag, to be brandished if the need ever arose.

During the same week in June when I was struggling through the Boat Crew School, the *Jeanie Johnston* was returning to Fenit from her almost-two-month stay in Cork. Fortunately, a local journalist, Peter Malone of *The Kerryman*, was aboard as a crew member, so there's a good record of what the voyage was like.

The crew, Peter reported, "have left wives and work at 24 hours' notice; some traveled down from Galway and Dublin. All are supporters of the *Jeanie Johnston* Project. They are managers, shopkeepers, bank officials and architects; there's an ex-mariner from the US Navy, a student of homeopathy, and a man who must be 80. Some are blue-water sailors; others have never been to sea in their lives."

Peter's diary traces the learning curve these amateur sailors went through, and there's a touch of awe at the responsibility thrust upon them: "Second Officer John Gill gathers the Mizzen Watch on the bridge to talk us through steering the ship. He seems entirely unconcerned at the thought of passing 500 tonnes of timber into the hands of us innocents."

Their first night at sea is "wet and blustery," Peter's watch awakes at 0800 to find the ship in Baltimore Harbor (close to the southernmost point of Ireland), where they'd put in to escape the weather. "Captain Mike Forwood," he wrote, "is playing careful with both ship and crew. One of the seams is also leaking, as the seams between the timbers on a wooden boat are sometimes wont to do. The leak quickly becomes a flood of rumour, and there are reports from shore that the *Jeanie Johnston* is sinking. This is news to everyone on board."

By 2300 the second night, the weather is deteriorating rapidly. "The ship's timbers creak as it resists the force of wind and water. Crockery crashes in the galley. The O'Regan brothers are up and down all night tending the ship they built."

The following morning is Sunday, and at 0800 Peter hears the Captain announce that all available hands are to get ready on deck "to worship." "After the night we've had," he writes, "it seems appropriate. The Fore and Main watches are knackered; some had to retire from deck as a squall reaching 50 knots hit west of the Skelligs. At breakfast a sailor aims milk at his cereal and ends up pouring it over the table. I ask the Captain if I might have a brief interview after the service. Mike Forwood bursts out laughing. 'We're going to wear ship, not worship!' he says. In short, we were going to turn it about."

Fleeing from a Force 9 gale (47-54 mph), they seek shelter in Brandon Bay, then make for their home port later in the day.

For the ship's crew, their first voyage had been a memorable one. For her partisans, the future was looking brighter. The *Jeanie Johnston* had not only passed all her tests and become the darling of the crowds; she had also proved her seaworthiness by weathering a great storm.

Now if only her human mentors could work out their differences, the tide and the force would be with her.

But Murphy and the leprechauns were not finished with her yet. They were lurking just around the corner, and toward the end of June they made their move.

"The **** has hit the fan here," said Helen's urgent email.

The event that had sent shock waves through the ranks of *Jeanie Johnston* supporters was an announcement by the Kerry Council Manager that he would advise the Council at their meeting four days hence not to assume ownership of the ship because certain promised financial arrangements had not been met. It appeared that what he feared were hidden debts the Council might inherit along with the ship.

"Since the Kerry Council is 60 percent responsible for the ship's debt," said Helen, "if they vote against the takeover, a receiver will most likely be brought in and the ship sold off to the highest bidder."

Padraig Kennelly, in *Kerry's Eye*, wrote that the Councilors would most likely vote with their Manager, since none would want to risk assuming personal liability for unspecified debts. There would then be two options: (1) The Jeanie Johnston Company would pay off its debts by finding a customer for the ship; "That," said Kennelly, "is as unlikely as finding a York-shire terrier taking the place of the Puck Goat at this year's Kill-orglin August Fair (Readers not from County Kerry can only guess at this allusion); or (2) The ship would be auctioned off.

"It's such a shame," said Helen, "just as the Project seemed to have turned a corner. Sorry to be the bearer of such bad tidings, but I know you want the truth, however unpalatable."

"Unpalatable" was hardly the word. It was unbearable. All the months-- actually years-- of packing, preparation, waiting and cheerleading had come to naught. My grand adventure had eluded me. My book-to-be was good for nothing but the scrap heap because it could never be completed.

For John Griffin, Mike Forwood and the others, who had literally devoted years of their lives to the Project, it had to be a devastating blow.

When I finally got over feeling sorry for myself and all the wonderful friends I'd made, I began to speculate on what might happen next. Who, I wondered, might buy the ship? Many would love to have her but few could afford to buy or keep her up. The worst-case scenario was probably the most likely: the ship would be bought by a Greek tycoon or perhaps by a Saudi prince--to be used strictly as a plaything.

I pictured a horrifying outcome. The Saudi prince sails his newly-acquired ship, Saudi flag flying from the masthead, into Boston Harbor. Thousands of irate Irish/American Bostonians, in a great roiling crowd, race to the waterfront, crowd into whatever boats are available and make their way to where the *Jeanie Johnston* (If, indeed, that is still her name) lies at anchor, board the ship, throw its owner overboard and hoist up the Irish flag. A latter-day Boston Tea Party.

Heaven forbid that it should ever come to that.

CHAPTER 11
The Last of the Leprechauns

Was it really all over?

The ship had already risen from the dead three times. Could she do it again? Or were the leprechauns about to triumph? Brendan Dinneen and the project's other officers had been told quite bluntly that the Council would be "pulling the plug on the Project." But they hadn't actually voted yet to do so. The vote was scheduled for the Council meeting on Monday, July 1.

At 8 a.m. on July 1, I called Helen Ryle. It was 1 p.m. in Ireland, and the Council meeting must be over. Helen said it wasn't. The meeting had started first thing in the morning and was still in progress.

Later in the day I called Brendan. The Council had voted, he said, but only to postpone their vote on the ownership question until July 15. There was now a two-week period in which something might be done to save the ship.

I suggested to Brendan that the only hope might be for a person-- or perhaps a consortium-- in the US to buy the ship and try to preserve the dream that launched it. Couldn't we contact leadership elements in the Irish/American community for help? Brendan had no objection. He'd already had an offer from America, he said, for 2 million euros-- far short of the amount needed to wipe out the debt.

But Turlough McConnell saw little hope in mounting such an effort. "They all have had no end of requests," he said, "but they didn't rise to the occasion." To carry sufficient weight, he believed, an appeal would have to come from the Irish Government, and he saw nothing developing in that quarter. Turlough convinced me I'd be spinning my wheels if I tried to alert and arouse the Irish/American community. I didn't have the time or the means to do it in any case.

Helen reported that public sentiment in Ireland now appeared to favor the ship: "Everybody agrees that the project is worthy and that the ship should sail to Dublin and Belfast this summer in preparation for a spring 2003 departure for the US, but no one can see where the money for this is to come from. I think it will have to be a private or corporate initiative."

Four hundred people had visited the ship the previous Sunday at its Fenit pier, she noted, "in the rain and at the same time the world cup soccer final and an important local county football game were on TV. So it's evident how much grass roots support there is for the Jeanie."

For two agonizing weeks I lived with the vague hope that something good might happen, and on July 15-- the very day of the deadline-- it did. An email from Helen told me that The Kerry Group, a large international food products company with its roots in Ireland, had stepped forward to propose forming a new partnership with the two Councils and Shannon Development--the three entities already in the picture--and the Kerry Council had voted to accept the proposal.

"They're each putting around 200,000 euros into the kitty," said Helen. "That will mean visiting Irish ports this summer and doing the US voyage next spring. Great news, eh?"

I read the message to Marie, and her reaction was immediate: "We need to celebrate. You've been at this for so long. It's time we heard some good news.

I told Helen we were breaking out a bottle of champagne, and she responded that she would be raising a pint of Guinness to us at the end of the day. The new entry on her web site that evening confirmed all she had told me and added that the Kerry Group's proposal described the *Jeanie Johnston* as "part of our country's heritage," and that while it was not possible to be definitive in the long term, they were proposing that the ship revisit Cork in the summer, then sail to Dublin and Belfast, and that "the 2003 programme should commence at the beginning of the year and would involve spending the full year in North America and visiting key centres there."

The Kerry Group were no strangers to the *Jeanie Johnston* project. Their Managing Director, Hugh Friel, was an ardent sailor and had taken a leading role in the Project from the beginning. Brendan Dinneen had been with the Kerry Group also, as Financial Controller and Head of Development, and the Kerry Group had been instrumental in having him join the *Jeanie Johnston* Project to try getting it back on the financial track.

Brendan told me all this when I called to find out what would be happening next. A new board of directors would be designated, he told me, and as soon as all arrangements were in place, the new company would take over the ship and guide her future. The Kerry Group would put up 200,000 euros, the two councils another 200,000, and Shannon Development would contribute by forgiving a 190,000 euro loan it had made. But Shannon was dragging its feet a bit.

The process would take time to play out, and there would have to be cooperation all around if it were to work smoothly. Brendan was hopeful, though somewhat weary. "We're all getting a bit cranky," he said. "Too many people are pushing us."

I told Brendan I'd have an opportunity to visit the ship again, and we made tentative plans to meet early in September. Marie and I would again be in Europe-- this time on a riverboat trip up the Rhine and down the Danube, from Amsterdam to Budapest. I was proposing that Marie fly home from Amsterdam while I go on to Ireland, as we had done two years earlier.

Now that there was hope in the air, the Irish press was striking a more positive note. "New Hope for *Jeanie Johnston*," proclaimed The *Kerryman*'s headline for an article that applauded the Kerry Group's move: "The best of luck to them; the company's involvement shows great civic spirit, and they deserve to benefit from it. But it would be too narrow a focus to assess the Project merely in cash terms. The *Jeanie Johnston* has provided an opportunity for young people from both sides of the border to work together, it has the potential to play a major role in tourism and it can be used for sail training. More than that, it might foster a sense of pride in our maritime past."

Padraig Kennelly, writing in *Kerry's Eye,* saw the Kerry Group's "name and integrity, plus their track record of doing things right first time" as "a very valuable item" in the new agreement. "There is a groundswell of public opinion," he added, "among the Tralee business people I have spoken to, that (the *Jeanie Johnston* Project) should be supported 'just one more time.'"

But until the i's were dotted and the t's crossed, red tape and bureaucracy were bogging down the ship's movements. During the heady days when she was opened to the public in Cork, a number of business leaders had been so impressed that they inquired about chartering the ship for brief periods. Out of those discussions came two charters-- one for Ford Motor Company for a week, and the other for a pilgrimage group going to Spain.

Getting permission from the Government was such a painfully slow process, though, that both charters had to be canceled. By the time approvals might have come through, it would have been too late to promote the events.

By mid-August the ship still had not moved from Fenit. Eager crowds awaited in port cities all along the Irish coast, and Brendan told me he was trying hard to accommodate them, but the convoluted approval process that would continue until the ship's new status was resolved made any movement virtually impossible.

We were coming up on our European trip, and I'd told Brendan I'd be flying from Amsterdam to Ireland on September 2. But where would the ship be at that time? In truth, no one knew. According to plan, she ought to be in Dublin, or perhaps Belfast. I worked out alternate ground itineraries. If she were still in Fenit, Brendan would have someone pick me up at Shannon Airport. If she were in Dublin, I'd bus to Limerick and take the train cross-country. I never worked out a Belfast itinerary, hoping I wouldn't have to.

The failure of Shannon Development to ratify the new agreement was now holding up all progress. The stage was set, the actors were psyched up to go on, and the audience was whistling for the show to start. All that was needed was for the last of the four partners to sign on.

"The biggest problem caused by Shannon," said Padraig Kennelly in *Kerry's Eye*, "is that it is holding up crew training and tours to other Irish ports. These will act as training voyages and based on them, will allow plans to be made to ensure the success of the 2003 US East Coast visit." The holdup also prevented the new company from meeting with the creditors, and that in turn prevented the Aquadome company, Tralee Waterworld, from starting construction of its new attraction in the former shipyard at Blennerville.

As we flew off on our European trip, those questions still hung in the air. It wasn't until somewhere toward the end of our Rhine/Danube voyage-- I think it was in Budapest-- that I was able to access my email and find a welcome message from Helen. It said Shannon Development had issued a statement in the past week agreeing to invest the money they had loaned, and that they "look forward to working closely with Kerry Group and the Kerry local authorities to ensure that the full potential of the Jeanie Johnston Project is realised."

Now that all parties were agreed, said Helen, the new

company could be formed and planning in earnest could begin for a voyage to Dublin and indeed for the proposed transatlantic voyage in early 2003.

Flying into Shannon Airport for the second time in two years, I recalled my rainy welcome on the first trip. This time the skies were clear and sunny, and I took that to be a good omen.

Mike Forwood himself picked me up at the airport, making me feel like a member of the inner circle. There was much to talk about on the drive down to Tralee, and as we passed sunny green fields sloping to the sea, old stone houses, timeless crossroads villages and ancient churches, I was torn between enjoying the loveliness of the countryside and listening to Mike's story of the trials of recent months.

"You can stay on the ship if you'd like," he said as we arrived at the Fenit pier. I had made no other plan so I stowed my gear in the bunk he indicated and followed him into the great cabin. Brendan and his wife Mary were waiting to greet me, and the first order of business was to break out a bottle of wine and toast the Jeanie. The fine dinner that followed was, they told me, the first ever served in the great cabin, and I felt greatly honored.

Later, there was a brief tour of the ship with Mike and then I was on my own to wander about and marvel at what I saw. The rigging was now complete in every detail. The tarpaulins and scaffolding were gone, and the deck houses stood on their own, sturdy and neat. The wood trim-- the railings, the ship's wheel, the massive dining table in the great cabin-- everything had been sanded, varnished and rubbed to perfection, and it shone with the shimmering beauty that can only be attained through hand labor.

While the ship had not yet made a major voyage, it had felt the footsteps of hundreds of people for more than two years, and a work crew were busy sanding the decks.

I roamed and pried, trying to discover all the ship's secrets.

Ciaran and Peter O'Regan were aboard, and I asked Ciaran to explain a puzzling anomaly-- an enclosed space between two bulkheads that didn't seem to be accounted for. "It's where the vent comes up from the tank room," he said.

Rounding a corner in the semidarkness below decks, I came face to face with a man in 19th century garb playing a fiddle. He seemed to be looking straight into my eyes, and it took a startled moment to realize this was one of John Griffin's theatrical props. I felt the need to reach out and touch him to make certain he wasn't real. Nearby I encountered a ragged urchin, probably a stowaway; a seasick man lying in a bunk attended by the ship's doctor; a woman sewing; and the stern-faced captain himself, his gaze directed downward as though studying a chart. Two years earlier, these figures had been sketches on a drawing board. Now they were electrifying realities.

I talked with members of the work crew who were taking a break. Gerard Diggins had a copy of *Ireland Afloat*. "Are you the man who wrote this letter about tourism?" he asked. I admitted I was, and this was the first I'd seen it. Another crew member, Jacinta Whelehan, was a young woman who told me she spent all her time aboard square-rigged ships wherever she could find them-- crewing, cooking, doing deck chores. "It's my life," she said simply.

A discussion arose among the group about the high-handed attitude of the Irish Government. "Why they can't give this ship more support, I don't know," said one. "You know why," said another. "It's because they can't stand the idea that a Kerryman thought of this project before they did. You know what they think of Kerrymen, and John Griffin is a Kerryman. They're just jealous."

The one thing I could learn nothing about was what I wanted most to know-- when the ship would sail to America. Mike still had his January sailing plan on the table, but neither he nor Brendan could say anything with certainty until the company newly formed to take over the ship got its act together and began planning in earnest.

As soon as I could, I called Helen Ryle. "You promised to buy me a Guinness," I told her, "and I'm here to collect it." We agreed to meet the following day, and Brendan and Mary joined us for a couple of hours at their favorite local pub. Helen was now doing, as a volunteer, the job the Project's web site should always have been doing, and Brendan was grateful.

Next day, Mike had to drive to Blennerville, to the old shipyard site, to pick up some equipment, and I went along. The detritus of history lay everywhere about. In the abandoned workshop, a huge shedlike building, materials left over from building the ship were gathering dust. There were long slabs of Austrian larch, lead ballast blocks, piles of lumber, boxes of bolts, lengths of pipe. The shipyard itself was filled with the remains of the great canopy that had provided shelter during the early construction days. It now lay in rusting piles of steel girders. In the unfinished and only partially occupied building that housed the Project's offices, my footsteps echoed down the long, empty hallways.

What had taken place there--whether an efficient, well-managed process or not-- had fulfilled a vision and produced something for the world to marvel at, and nothing could take that away from the ship's creators and builders.

On the last day of my visit, Brendan invited me to a Rotary luncheon in Tralee. Rotary luncheons look pretty much alike everywhere in the world, and if it hadn't been for the lilting, sometimes dialect-heavy speech, I might have been in the US.

Brendan told our tablemates about the upcoming voyage and my part in it. A bright-eyed man introduced to me as a local mortician leaned across the table: "Do you mean to tell me that you're going to cross the Atlantic on a wooden boat?" When I said I intended to, he whipped out his business card, handed it to me with a smile and said "Tom, there's not a thing to worry about. As long as you've got your American Express card, I can ship you home."

He was only kidding, Brendan assured me on the way back.

There was one more thing I wanted to do before leaving Ireland. Less than five miles from where the ship lay at its pier in Fenit were the ruins of the ancient Ardfert Cathedral, a site associated with St. Brendan the Navigator, who founded a monastery there in the 6th century. St. Brendan had long occupied a place in my mind as a pivotal figure in the *Jeanie Johnston* Project, and I felt I somehow had to make contact with him.

He was, first of all, the Irish patron saint of sailors, and Marie had given me a St. Brendan medal to wear on the voyage. He was born in 484 in Fenit, where the ship was now berthed. And from the Irish point of view, he was the explorer who discovered America almost 1,000 years before Columbus.

A famous medieval manuscript, the *Navigatio Sancti Brendani,* describes St. Brendan's voyages in boats made of ox-hides, including one on which he discovered a land far to the west of Ireland. It was recorded in medieval times as an island, but there has been speculation in more recent years that what St. Brendan discovered was the continent of North America.

He began his voyage in Brandon Bay, just around the bend from Tralee Bay and no more than 10 miles from Fenit, and the Feast of St. Brendan on May 16 is still celebrated in Kerry by climbing Mt. Brandon, which rises just behind the bay. Marie and I had followed the ancient track called "The Saint's Path" to the summit during our Irish walking tour in 1998, not realizing then that it had such significance.

The Irish belief that their man and not Columbus discovered America was once dismissed as a mere pub boast, but in 1977 explorer Tim Severin proved it could be done by sailing an ox-hide boat 3,500 miles from Brandon Bay to Newfoundland, using the ancient Latin text itself as his boat-building guide. Then a boulder was found in Newfoundland inscribed with what some scholars believe is ogham, an ancient Irish form of

143

writing that Christian monks are known to have used in the 5th and 6th centuries. The Ardfert site also had an ogham stone.

I took a taxi out to Ardfert and asked the driver to wait. No one else was there. I walked on green turf through the roofless interior of the cathedral, looked up at the soaring lancet windows, studied an imposing Celtic cross in the graveyard and meditated beside the ogham stone. The sky was gray and the acres of stone ruins were gray, but the day for me had taken on a mystic color, and I went away feeling I had made a connection.

A month went by after my return from Ireland, and then another month, with no word from anyone about the *Jeanie Johnston*. Early in November, I emailed Brendan and fortunately caught him just before he was to go on two weeks' leave.

"At a creditors' meeting on October 25," he said, "we got unanimous approval of a scheme of arrangement." The company's creditors had agreed to accept a 60 percent repayment of their investments, and all that was needed now was the High Court's approval of the arrangement.

There were still plans to get the ship to Dublin and Belfast before Christmas and plans for the North American voyage were in the works, though they couldn't yet be finalized.

But this progress was not without its sacrifices. John Griffin was still on suspension, the investigation was under way, and Mike Forwood was no longer there. "The new regime wants to start with a clean sheet," was the way Brendan put it.

This was shocking news. Mike had given the project his best for three years and was now to be denied the triumph of commanding the ship on its Atlantic voyage. I was too far away to know who was making the decisions and how they were being made. If I wished to continue with the *Jeanie Johnston*, I would have to accept the fact that there would be a new captain. I was committed to the voyage and would surely do that, but in the meantime I was deeply upset over this development.

144

Toward the end of November, the ship sailed back to Cork for adjustments to its masts and rigging, and it was opened to the public again at the dock. Helen reported that from Cork it would sail to Dublin and then Belfast for sail training, maintenance and final rigging. Her bush telegraph was telling her that the new CEO would most likely be Denis Reen, CEO of the Aquadome, who had bought the Blennerville shipyard.

On December 12, Helen posted the kind of news we had all been waiting for-- the itinerary for the coming months with specific hours and dates. The ship had already left for Dublin, where it would be open to the public until January 5. It would be open in Belfast on the 18th and 19th, in Waterford from January 25 to February 2, and back in Tralee from February 8 to 14. On Sunday, February 16, the Jeanie would sail from Tralee, stop in Tenerife, in the Canaries, from March 8 until March 13, then sail for America, arriving at a US southern port as yet unchosen on April 17. Between these engagements, there would be further sea trials in the Irish Sea.

"The Kerry Group have put their boot under the Project and kick-started it," Helen told me. "There was an hour's coverage on national radio today with interviews onboard with the new captain, Tom McCarthy, who comes across very well."

Five days later, the official word came from the new CEO, Denis Reen, in an email message addressed to the Friends of the *Jeanie Johnston*: "The scheme of arrangement proposed by Kerry Group was sanctioned by the court today. This allows the new board, under the chairmanship of Hugh Friel, to assume responsibility for the Jeanie Johnston. The CEO of the new company will be myself, Denis Reen."

Enclosed was a letter from Captain Tom McCarthy with a schedule of voyage dates, a berth application and medical questionnaire. Captain McCarthy, a native of County Cork, had been Captain of the *Asgard II*, Ireland's national sail training ship, for nine years, taking her to Australia and the US. More recently he had captained the *Lord Nelson* and *Tenacious*.

Finally, after three years, there was a specific sailing date, officially published-- February 16 from Tralee. Would February's weather be any different from that of January? I went back to my storm track data, which showed we had a 40 percent chance of encountering storms in January between Ireland and the Canaries. There were no comparable data for February, so I preferred to believe the odds would be even better. Little did I know that Murphy and the leprechauns were to have one last fling before we escaped their clutches for good.

There were still some arrangements to be made-- rigging my laptop computer for the voyage, working out details of how I would transmit stories via the ship's satellite telex system, presenting the Coast Guard Auxiliary plaque prior to the sailing. In a brief phone conversation with Captain McCarthy, I caught a bit of personal philosophy that sounded attractive. "Once we know what we're doing," he said, "and we have safety considerations fully in place, I believe our next goal should be enjoyment."

As I filled out my berth application and medical questionnaire (once again) I mused on the trials and near-disasters of the past three years that had given way finally to this moment of triumph. The battle had been won, and the victory was sweet. The thought of the voyage at that moment seemed almost anti-climactic, though I knew that once the ship moved out from the dock it would assume a glorious momentum of its own.

I couldn't resist returning to *Ulysses*. Lines I hadn't dwelt on earlier now leapt out at me: *"How dull it is to pause, to make an end, to rust unburnished, not to shine in use!"*. . .*"Life piled on life were all too little, and of one to me little remains"*. . .*"this gray spirit yearning in desire to follow knowledge like a sinking star, beyond the utmost bound of human thought"*. . .*"There lies the port; the vessel puffs her sail; there gloom the dark, broad seas"*. . .*" 'Tis not too late to seek a newer world, push off, and sitting well in order smite the sounding furrows."*

Once again, I was ready. This time it might happen.

146

Above: The *Jeanie Johnston* in mid-Atlantic as crew members photograph her from the ship's rescue boat. *Below (L):* Statue of The Child of Prague in a niche in aft companionway. *Below (R):* Clergymen bless the ship before the voyage.

Above (L): Deck talks on navigation, sail handling and other aspects of the ship are given during the voyage. *Above (R):* Bosun's mate Dave Nolan was nimble as a monkey aloft. *Below:* Holding to a course in rough weather is a challenge.

Above: Footropes give crew members a place to stand as they furl sails. *Below (L):* Practice at boarding the rescue boat is good emergency training. *Below (R):* Lines, sheets, halyards and hawsers-- they're all rope, and they all need upkeep.

Above (L): John Gill uses his sextant and his 50 years of sea experience to teach celestial navigation. *Above (R):* The bosun's store, the ship's pint-size do-it-yourself center. *Below:* The little black dots show where we were day by day.

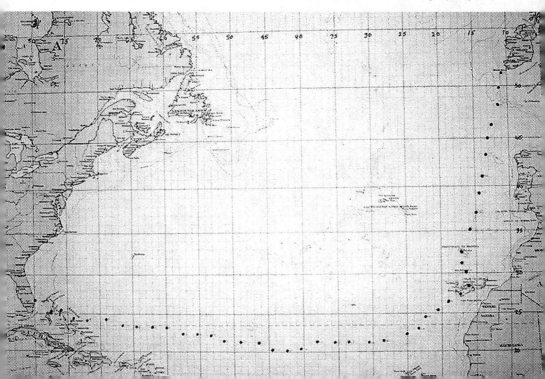

Above: Capt. Tom McCarthy, Engineer Peter O'Regan and First Officer Rob Matthews resolve a problem. *Below (L):* In Tenerife, Peter and Ciaran O'Regan confer on work priorities. *Below (R):* Bosun Tom Harding with the big catch.

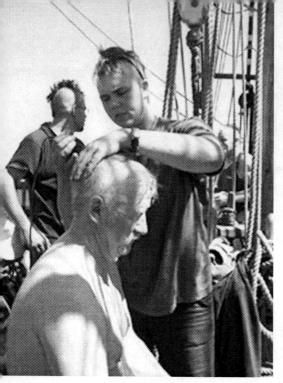

Above (L): Frida gives Capt. McCarthy his "Tropic of Cancer" haircut. She and Dave already have theirs. *Above (R):* Dining on deck in "trade wind" weather. *Below:* Relaxing time on deck; but who do those extra legs and feet belong to?

Above (L): St. Patrick's Day brought out musical talents. Watch Leader Frida Bjorsell toots a lilting tune. *Above (R):* Deck chores are always waiting for those willing to learn. *Below:* Looking at white water during one of the gales.

Above (L): The pilot comes aboard to guide us into port. *Above (R):* Tom Harding touches up the bowsprit. *Below (L):* The author, the only American aboard, takes the wheel as the ship enters US waters. *Below (R):* Time to leave.

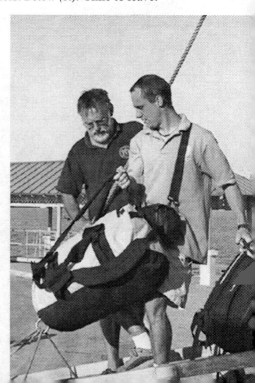

THE GRAND VOYAGE

PROLOGUE

The craic was mighty in Bailey's Corner Pub. Conversation had already reached high-decibel levels when the fiddlers finished tuning up and launched into a jig, and now Gary the publican was holding forth on the *Jeanie Johnston* Project. "People have been too critical," he was saying. "We've got to give the ship a chance. It's a grand idea, and when she sails, she'll be sailing into history." Mel Davidson, Pat McGrath and I, as signed-on crew members, pleasantly agreed. "I want a picture of the crew up here on my wall," Gary went on, and we saw ourselves immortalized among the politicians, cult figures and sports luminaries who make up Bailey's decor.

We three, along with other prospective crew members, were in Tralee five days ahead of the February 16 sailing date to undergo personal survival training. A pint or two at day's end helped relieve the somber nature of the instruction.

We had been told that day that for people not used to cold water (less than 60 degrees F), sudden immersion could bring on two problems-- cold shock or hypothermia-- either of which could result in death by drowning. It wasn't reassuring to learn that Irish fishermen purposely avoid learning to swim because they don't want to prolong the agony if they fall overboard.

Mel, a retired physics professor from Bellingham, Washington; and Pat, a retired businessman from Northern Ireland, are sailors, both with considerably more experience than I, and we were all taking the lessons seriously. Some of the material was familiar to me from my US Coast Guard Auxiliary training.

A full day in the classroom taught us how to abandon ship should that become a necessity; how to inflate and launch a life raft; distress signals and how to use them; helicopter rescue techniques (not too useful for us because we'd be out of helicopter range for most of the voyage); and the fine points of getting into and wearing immersion suits.

I recorded some highlights in my notebook: "cleanliness and hygiene essential. . .efficiency (don't be late on watch). . .Captain can discipline you, or put you ashore. . .death at sea: corpse in freezer, or helicoptered off. . .can question orders, but can't disobey. . .voyage crew won't be forced to go aloft. . .the worst thing is loss of privacy."

A roster was passed around asking for names, dates of birth and other basic information. I noted that there were a handful of seniors in our group, but most of the crew were in their teens, 20s and 30s. At the next break, a man who appeared to be in his late 60s approached me with a quizzical look. "It says on the roster that you were born in 1921," he said. "Could that be true?" That was how Pat McGrath and I met, and we became friends on the spot.

A large part of another day was spent in the pool of the Tralee Aquadome. "Get into clothes you don't mind getting wet," said the instructor, "and empty your pockets of anything you don't want dunked."

Then, wearing life jackets, we jumped into the pool in the prescribed manner-- feet first, one hand protecting the nose and the other holding the life jacket down, swam across the pool and arranged ourselves into a water-borne classroom, treading

148

water while the instructor gave the balance of his lesson.

Squirming into the immersion suits required hard work and acrobatics, but their promise of warmth and dryness was reassuring. We jumped in, swam and drifted; then, one at a time, hauled ourselves up a short ladder into the 20-man life raft that floated nearby. It was hard to imagine 20 people crammed into the claustrophobic interior with its rubbery, unstable floor, and the thought that popped into my mind was, "I hope we never have to use one of these."

Our last chore, at the conclusion of the survival course, was to sign on for the voyage. The Government form made clear that we were "seamen" and for the duration of the voyage would be under the jurisdiction of the Irish Merchant Marine. The Captain, under law, is fully responsible for everything that happens on his ship, and in consequence he has total command of everything, including the crew. When we signed the ship's articles, we were pledging obedience to the Captain-- and agreeing to the consequences if there were to be disciplinary action. The form referred to the Maritime Act of 1906, and I was glad to see that the disciplinary measures in force were fines only; flogging, apparently, was no longer allowed.

Time passed quickly in Tralee. There was last-minute shopping to be done, and I had a warm-hearted, pleasant dinner with Helen Ryle and after-dinner drinks with her and her husband.

At the Tralee Town House, where Pat, Mel and I were staying, along with Jim O'Brien of Dublin, concerns began to mount as the sailing date approached. We were to report aboard ship on Saturday, in preparation for a Sunday departure, and there were still unanswered questions about what and how much gear to take aboard. A sail trainee in our survival course, who had been on one of the *Jeanie Johnston*'s Irish coastal voyages, had told us there was a bare minimum of stowage space for individual crew members.

"I have the phone number of the ship," I volunteered. "Why

don't I call the Captain and ask if one of us can come aboard briefly and check out the stowage?"

While I waited for Captain McCarthy to come on the line, I heard a jumble of voices. I sensed pressure and tension. Departure checklists, no doubt, and last-minute stores coming aboard.

He heard me out, then said, "We're too busy here. Bring your gear aboard, and if there's too much we'll just have to put the excess off on the dock."

Direct, hard, no nonsense. Was that what the voyage was going to be like?

That information-- or lack of it-- led to some frantic repacking. I reduced two duffle bags to one and arranged to mail the excess gear home.

Brendan Dinneen picked us up at noon on Saturday and drove us to the dock at Fenit. The ship, sturdy and proud, was the only unmoving object on the scene. Trucks and hand carts were being wheeled about. Vendors and crew members staggered over the gangway laden with boxes and bags while others checked and signed for deliveries. A set of what we presumed to be spare wooden spars were being manhandled from dock to deck.

As we stood on the dock, a powerful wind was blowing out of a cloudy sky, presaging a possibly stormy start for our voyage.

At 1330 we boarded the ship and were given our bunk and watch assignments. My bunk was the top one in a spare two-bunk compartment forward of the main mess deck. Other than a slim hanging locker and some slots beneath the lower bunk, I could see no storage space.

My bunk mate, 68-year-old Jim Callery, and I looked at each other and agreed we were in trouble. Jim had even more gear than I had.

We split the space in the hanging locker, stowed what we could in niches and crannies and sent the rest to dead storage in

150

some subterranean bilge space.

There followed in quick succession brief welcoming talks by the Captain and First Officer Rob Matthews, stressing the need for order, safety and cleanliness; a familiarity lecture on sails and their halyards, lines and sheets; and a practice session bracing the yards in what was now a chilling wind.

In the late afternoon it was time for a long-scheduled event-- my presentation of the US Coast Guard Auxiliary plaque to the Captain. We were both in uniform for the occasion, and as we shook hands for the photographer, he leaned close and said, "I'm sorry I was a bit brusque with you on the phone a couple of days ago."

"Don't think of it," I said. "I know you've been under great pressure." With that, we seemed to have healed whatever breach there was.

When Jim and I climbed into our bunks that night, we little realized that it would be many nights before we would have a stable sleep again in a reasonably stationary bed.

DAY 1
Sunday, 16 February

There are days in our youth when the world is still bright and unblemished and almost anything seems possible. Today-- at least the first half of it-- came close to being such a day.

We'd settled in, met the ship's officers and watch leaders and had a general idea of what we were about. Now the bright windy morning was spent cleaning up, coiling ropes, doing last-minute touchups for the departure ceremony.

I thought back over the past three uncertain years and reached the heady conclusion that no one or nothing was likely at this point to pluck me off the ship. For the *Jeanie Johnston* and me, it was at last a GO.

Reporters and television crews came aboard after lunch and

anyone standing about was interviewed three or four times. By 2 p.m. invited guests were filling seats on the dock and the Army band started playing. I saw John Griffin on the dock, waved to him and tried to remind him, in words and pantomime, that none of this would have happened without him.

The bishops and politicians boarded and joined the Captain on the quarterdeck for greetings and speeches Some of the words could be heard but the wind carried many away. The air was full of carnival spirit.

After the last of the speeches, the Kerry flag was run up the ship's flag halyard, then the Irish flag, and finally we cast off to great cheers from the crowd.

When we left the Fenit pier, we knew, long before the escort fleet turned back, that the weather was building. As we passed Brandon Bay the wind turned against us. Square sails came down and we powered for the rest of the afternoon and through the night, under bare poles, straight into the teeth of a Force 9 (47-54 mph) gale with Force 10 (55-63 mph) gusts.

There was no place to sit, stand or lie steadily. The ship pitched as much as she rolled. Every loose thing slid, slithered or rolled. Each time the ship dropped between waves, the anchor chains smashed against the inside of the hawse pipes, sending a loud metallic "clang" through all the living spaces.

All but three aboard were sick, and I was not one of the three. I spent 12 hours in my bunk, braced against the rolling, wondering if I would live or die.

DAY 2
Monday, 17 February

In the rough and confused seas, we were making little progress, and with seasickness now endemic, the Captain decided to seek shelter. He called us together in the mess deck and tried to be reassuring. We would try to find refuge behind Valencia Island, across Dingle Harbor on the Kerry Peninsula.

Through our weariness there was a hint of euphoria, because, strangely, we were all still alive. "In all my voyage experience," said the Captain, "I've hardly ever known the first case of seasickness to repeat itself. And my aim is not to give you another night like last night."

A tall ship is a big target, and there are few places where you can hide it. That's been our problem. It's not an enemy we are trying to hide from but the wind.

We tried anchoring off Knights Town on Valencia Island, but the anchor didn't hold, and we tried again and again.

At lunchtime we heard the windlass grinding and someone said, "Sounds like we're moving again." "Yes," said another, "they're trying to get us closer to the pub." But no such luck. There was no way off the ship in any case.

For fear we might continue to drag anchor and not have enough sea room for maneuver, we abandoned the harbor. There was some thought that we might go back across the bay and shelter in Dingle Harbor, but the Captain couldn't see going into a small harbor where he'd sacrifice maneuverability. So we ran up the coast to get behind the high cliffs on the south side of Dingle Bay.

That didn't work either. The wind was now coming over the cliffs in hurricane-force bursts, and we started to drag anchor again. Bosun Tom Harding hauled the anchor in pitch darkness with the wind screaming in the rigging.

The only thing to do was to keep moving, and we did.

DAY 3
Tuesday, 18 February

All last night and all day today, we have been a Flying Dutchman, powering back and forth in Dingle Bay under the lee of its south shore, reversing our course every four hours and getting no closer to Tenerife, or anywhere else for that matter. There is nothing to do but wait, and we have proved that this is the only way we can do it.

We've been getting to know one another better now that we are no longer all sick together. Jim Callery has proved to be a fount of information on the potato famine, and we have had the first of many conversations about it. Jim, a successful Irish businessman, is the founder of the National Famine Museum in Strokestown, Ireland.

The professional crew are coming into focus for us, too. Bosun Tom Harding had said we might need to put into La Coruna, near the northwestern tip of Spain, in the event we had to refuel, and I asked him how long it might take to get there. "At the speed we've been doing," he said, "it might take a week." This fruitless driving full power into the wind is burning fuel fast, and we can't afford to do it indefinitely.

Tom is the perfect type-cast bosun-- short, stocky, strong as an ox, totally at ease with everyone above or below his station, an unlimited source of sea stories and always a ready laugh. He's such a perfect type, in fact, he was invited to play the role of Captain Jack Aubrey's bosun in the forthcoming movie of Patrick O'Brian's novel, *HMS Surprise*. But a long-awaited berth on an Antarctic voyage came along and he took it instead.

After two days, word has come back to us that some of the Irish press are being quite unkind. "*Jeanie Johnston* Heads Back Home" was one of the headlines, and the story implied the ship was giving up the voyage.

We are all seething about this. The fact is, the Captain had no choice. With a fixed sailing date, you can only take what comes, and what came was well forecast-- a huge storm system moving up from the southeast. All we could do was plow our way into it, and then try to wait it out. When he has time on his side, the Captain will be able to avoid bad weather or wait for it to ease.

DAY 4
Wednesday, 19 February

By early this morning, the wind was down to Force 7 (32-38 miles per hour) and back in the southeast, so the Captain decided to make a run for it out of Dingle Bay and get our voyage properly started. Today is brisk and sunny, and if we alter our course to the west, we can sail by this wind. The huge seas-- 20 feet and more-- are still running after yesterday's storm.

Sunrise brought us abreast of the Skelligs, those jagged rocks off the coast where hardy Irish monks once lived in isolation from the world. Most sails have been set and we are motor-sailing to make as much speed as possible. The Captain has made it clear he wants to escape these stormy latitudes.

This is a good day to sit on the high side of the mess table. Sitting high, the ship's heel holds you against the table, and any food you spill goes to your neighbors across the way. Sit on the low side and you'll have to hang on by your fingernails to the table's edge, and chances are you'll end up with someone's soup in your lap.

It's also a good day, when you're off duty, to put on your deck boots and warm one-piece deck suit, go on deck, lash the tether on your safety harness to something solid and enjoy the ship and the sea. You can take deep breaths of clean Atlantic air, study the habits of the graceful gannets wheeling overhead, or turn your face to the sickly, storm-hidden sun. From time to time, bursts of white water sluice across the deck at your feet.

The weather report is not good. A southerly gale is expected again tonight, and the coming week, according to the weather fax received in the wheel house, looks much the same, with one southerly gale after another.

Going to bed means climbing into our bunks-- sometimes at

great peril; tying in place the canvas lee sheet designed to keep us from rolling out, and hoping for sleep.

DAY 5
Thursday, 20 February. Position at 1530: 48-06 N, 11-42 W

We are making good time today-- between 6 and 7 knots. As the Captain notes, however, our twin 280-hp diesels are auxiliary engines, not intended to fully power a 540-ton ship. We are consuming fuel at a rapid rate and may have to put in to Lisbon or Madeira to refuel.

This day has been sunny but rough, as high swells from the west collide with lesser swells from the southeast. The result is confusing seas and a great deal of rolling.

With the exaggerated motion of the ship and the noise of the engines and anchor chains, we've had very little sleep. Being partly asleep and partly awake breeds hallucinatory dreams and fantasies and many of us are talking about these.

For me, it has reawakened a fantasy I've long had about footprints. Put this one down, I suppose, to a fascination with times long past.

In all the years I worked in New York, I must have left thousands of footprints on the streets of Manhattan. Wouldn't it be rewarding if they were outlined or rendered in some singular color that was visible to my eyes only? What I wouldn't give if I could retrace some of their long-ago meanderings.

The seas, too, have their footprints, if only we could see them, and the area we are traversing-- from Ireland to the Canaries-- would, if my fantasies were realized, be richly paved with the footprints of historic ships. Perhaps they would take the form of golden tracks on the surface of the sea.

Somewhere in the first hours of our voyage, we would have crossed an ancient track-- that of St. Brendan striking out boldly from the Dingle Peninsula for Iceland, Greenland and

156

perhaps North America. And now, opposite the English Channel, the surface is criss-crossed with scores of tracks-- John Cabot, in 1497, voyaging to Newfoundland; and Verrazano, sailing under a French commission, on his way to discover New York. Standing on our deck, I can imagine their passing us on the way out. Anywhere off our bow might be the outgoing track of the *Golden Hind*, as Sir Francis Drake sets off on his voyage round the world in 1577, and his incoming track three years later. Even now, we may be crossing Champlain's 1604 track to the St. Lawrence, or the 1609 track of Henry Hudson, on his way to discover for Europeans the coast of my native New Jersey and the great river nearby now named for him. And within the next few hours we must cross the track of Captain James Cook's *Endeavor,* off to discover the Pacific.

This little voyage, too, is laden with history, and in our small way we may be leaving our own golden track.

DAY 6
Friday, 21 February. Noon position: 46-39 N, 12-30 W

The day started with a bang. The wind is coming out of the southeast again, and by breakfast time it was up to Force 9 (47-54 mph). We are hove to against the gale and not making more than two or three knots.

Just as the 4 to 8 watch came off duty, the ship gave a huge lurch, followed by the sound of crockery smashing in the galley. Sarah Caffery the cook and her galley crew deserve every medal-- carrying crocks and tureens of food through two steel doors and down a slippery companionway three times a day, then trying to secure them on the mess table so we can get fed before they slide away.

I wonder if anyone has tried to work out a formula that would relate the viscosity of the porridge to the angle of the ship's roll.

If the porridge is not viscous enough, and the bowl is too full, it sloshes out on the table with the first roll. Soup is even worse. In the 19th century British Royal Navy, they thickened porridge and soup with crumbled ship's biscuit to avoid this problem-- but then you had weevils in your soup.

The crew were battened down below most of the day, and the only really safe place was in our bunks. But what do you do in your bunk? There's not enough overhead space to hold up a book, and radio reception is poor. The ship's motion won't let you sleep, so you end up dozing and going into a reverie.

Jim Callery, on his way to the head, took a nasty fall and cracked several ribs. He has considerable pain, and Tom McCormack, the ship's doctor, is attending him.

DAY 7
Saturday, 22 February. Position at 1500: 43-06 N, 13-08 W

Many of us were sick again, and the ship was a mess, but better times are coming. The wind has shifted to the west at Force 7 (32-38 mph), and we've set courses and topsails (the biggest sails) on main and foremasts.

The difference inside the ship is profound. The pitching and rolling have moderated and there's now a steady heel to port. The trouble is, the wind doesn't hold; in a few hours those sails may do us no good and will need to come down.

The big picture is that there's been a huge high pressure system over Europe, and we have been clawing our way down its western flank, fighting against its clockwise wind. We're now enough out in the open to catch a west wind, and with the help of the engines we're moving at nine knots.

Captain McCarthy observes that the weather pattern in the Atlantic is different than he has ever seen it in his 32 years at sea. In normal course, he says, the Bermuda-Azores high should be spinning us to the southwest via the wind along its edge, but that's not happening.

DAY 8

Sunday, 23 February. Noon position: 43-33 N, 13-28 W

Yesterday's position put us roughly opposite Bordeaux and about 250 miles northwest of La Coruna, Spain, earlier considered a possible port of refuge, though it now appears that we won't be stopping there.

Last night the Captain called us together in the mess deck and congratulated us on seeing the ship through the roughest time it's had in its young life. He showed our chart location and expressed the hope that we might be making landfall in Madeira in about three days.

Madeira wasn't on the schedule originally; we were to go straight to Tenerife, in the Canaries. But wisdom dictates that the ship be inspected after what it's been through and have its rigging tuned if necessary.

Some minor repairs and replacements may be needed as well. Our semi-rigid inflatable boat, carried on a davit off the stern, was smashed into uselessness during one of the gales by huge seas coming up beneath it and will have to be replaced.

Still another reason for stopping is to give the crew a respite. As Bosun Tom Harding puts it, "We are tired of this phase and crave some sunshine and calm seas. We are also thirsty for a few cold beers on terraced bars."

After the meeting, the Captain opened the bar in the great cabin, and we all enjoyed Murphy's Stout. A crew member brought out his guitar and gave us some Irish ballads, and the "craic," as they call it in Ireland, was great.

This morning a practice drill called all hands on deck. When we hear the alarm now we know we must put on life preservers and move fast. First Officer Rob Matthews then handed out survival suits and helped us get into them. These are complete

159

body suits, covering all but the face, and they are engineered to keep one alive and afloat in cold water for a considerable time. We hope we never have to use them but we are glad to be prepared.

DAY 9
Monday, 24 February. Position at 1530: 41-10 N, 13-53 W

The ship is talking to Peter O'Regan. As we toil through these steep and difficult seas, Peter roams from bow to stern, listening to the timbers groan and shift. "They're doing exactly what we expect them to do," he says. To Peter, a wooden ship is a living thing, and he understands its language: "The timbers are always 'working.' That's the way wooden ships are. All the wooden parts are constantly adjusting, finding new relationships with one another." If one of the relationships is not working out well, Peter's practiced ear warns him that this is an area to watch carefully. But at this point he seems satisfied with the music that reaches his ears from this symphony of creaking beams.

Peter and his brother Ciaran were the Jeanie Johnston's principal builders, as chief engineer and shipwright superintendent respectively, and Peter knows every nut and bolt on the ship.

In a deck talk today, he led us through the steps he followed in the ship's construction. "Everything about wooden shipbuilding," says Peter, "is about the eye. The builder arrives at his shapes more by sighting than by formal geometry. It's what we call getting 'a fair curve.'"

More than 75 percent of the Irish oak used for the frames came from trees downed by a storm in the Killarney National Forest, and he worked the wood green. "It would take forever to dry," he says, "and then it would swell and change shape when the ship was put in the water."

160

It took us a while to learn that the decks are hosed every morning not just for cleanliness but also to keep the deck planking swollen so the seams remain tight. This is a double-edged sword, however, because hosing causes some water to leak through. The larger truth is that if the wood were allowed to dry out, the seams would open and much more water would leak through from rain and heavy seas.

The seas are still rough, and we had rain today. Our present latitude is about 41 degrees, and Madeira is at about 33, so at 60 nautical miles per degree, we have some 480 miles to go. We all know now that our landfall port in the US will be West Palm Beach, and we hope our families can greet us there.

Volunteers are working with Bosun's mate Dave Nolan on jobs the voyage has shown a need for-- more handgrips for the cooks, a rope over the mess table so we can hold on with one hand and eat with the other, overhead ropes to steady ourselves when walking and a way of silencing the anchor chains.

DAY 10
Tuesday, 25 February. Position at 1400: 39-29 N, 14-38 W

Last night was possibly the worst yet, with very little sleep, but the view on deck this morning was full of promise. For more than a week there have been gray, rainy skies and steep, frothing seas. Today there are moderate swells, just short of breaking. The sky and the sea are pure blue. And the sun! It's no longer an Irish sun but a Spanish sun.

This could almost be a summer sea off our New Jersey coast, and we hope it marks the beginning of a new phase in the voyage.

The chief topic of conversation among the seniors on the mess deck last night was whether people like us are adventurous or crazy. In the end, we concluded that we're all a bit of each-- and there's no age limit to it.

161

Jim Callery thought that at 68 he was pushing the edge of the envelope. Then Jim O'Brien of Dublin, with about 30 years of merchant marine service behind him, was sure that at 74 he was the oldest crazy man. When he learned I was 81, he was crestfallen. Now when I see him at the mess table, I put my arm around his shoulder and say, "I think I'll sit here next to my son."

DAY 11
Wednesday, 26 February. Position at 9 am: 37-05 N, 14-54 W

Last night was relatively smooth, and that brought much-needed sleep to all hands, but now we have 15- to 20-foot swells coming in under our starboard quarter, making for a rolly ship. So rolly, in fact, that a couple of rogue waves came over the top of the forward deck house this morning and doused everyone on deck as they poured down. This is a new condition for us-- clear, sunny weather but steep, heavy seas.

For a while, there was a good northwest wind, but then the wind went against us again and the seas became confused. With staysails and spanker (all our fore-and-aft sails) up, and with help from the engines, we are making as much as seven knots.

One of our bow lookouts spotted a solitary puffin in the water just ahead of us. Tom Harding described the encounter: "He dived to escape our seething bow wave. He looked as startled to meet us as we were to encounter him 250 miles west of Lisbon. What he was doing, all alone, in such an agony of an ocean I cannot imagine, but he looked furtive and guilty when he dived with such suspicious alacrity."

The puffin was an anomaly. A central fact of our existence, of which we are all aware, is that we're alone. For 11 days, other than the puffin, no one has seen a ship, a bird, a fish, a whale, a dolphin or any other sign of life. A long, low silhouette far off our port side may have been a tanker, but that's all.

This sense of isolation binds us together. We turn to one another for companionship, for affirmation of our humanity. Each of us places a heightened value on all the others, for without them we'd be truly alone.

This is, after all, a small ship on a large ocean. On a calm day, it's no more than 40 paces on the deck from bow to stern.

That means, too, that whatever happens anywhere on the ship, we are all quickly aware of it. After one of our recent rough nights plowing through a gale, the word went around that the Captain had ordered an axe and a pair of wire cutters brought to the bridge. If a mast came down, he wanted the wreckage cleared away quickly before it could damage the hull.

DAY 12
Thursday, 27 February. Position at 0900: 35-11 N, 15-54 W

Very high swells on our beam made it a rolly night, and the lack of sleep is affecting all hands. People curl up on deck during the day wherever they can find a folded sail or something else reasonably soft, hoping to catch a half-hour nap; and it's not unusual to see others at the mess table, head down on folded arms and sound asleep. But today is a large day, full of warm sunshine and soft breezes, and that helps.

This morning at 0900 we were 162 nautical miles from Funchal, Madeira, and Rob, the first officer, says we should be there by about 1400 tomorrow.

The big news came when one of the watches yelled down to the mess deck, "Dolphins off the bow!" All hungry for a sign of life, we raced to the bow and watched, spellbound, as four dolphins cavorted just ahead of our bow wave, weaving about, leaping and darting.

Last night's mess deck conversation reminded me of Willie and Joe, Bill Mauldin's famous cartoon characters of World

War II. "When we get to Madeira," said one, "I'm going to hop into a bed that isn't moving, lie there for a while and savor its motionlessness, then sleep for a whole night without a lee sheet holding me in, and wake up in the morning to find the bed still level."

"I'm going to spend a whole day soaking in the shower," said another (Showers are usually off limits at sea; they're the most likely place, next to the galley, in which to break a bone or two).

"First thing I'm going to do," said another, is just stand for a few hours with my hands in my pockets and not worry about being knocked ass over teakettle."

This gave rise, naturally, to a philosophical discussion of the relative merits of stability vs. cleanliness. If you could have only one, which would you take?

When you're unstable, you could be hurt, so it might be better to be dirty but stable. On the other hand, you could offend your companions if you're dirty, so clean might be better. The negatives boil down to danger vs. loneliness. The majority voted for cleanliness, putting companionship above safety-- an interesting commentary on life at sea.

DAY 13
Friday, 28 February. Position at 1000: 32-40 N, 16-41 W

Early this morning, Madeira loomed off our starboard bow, appearing first as clumps of jagged hilly islets, resolving finally into a long mountainous main island with several small satellites. No one could resist longing glances. To a man (and a woman), we are ready for it. Our date with the pilot is at 1400, so we have time to kill motoring slowly outside Funchal Harbor.

Before the voyage, sailing purists said, "You won't be using the engines, will you, except in an emergency?" Well, the whole 1,200-nautical-mile run from Fenit to Madeira was an emergency. If we hadn't used the engines we might still be sitting in Dingle Bay.

Many an engineless 19th century famine ship spent three or more weeks tacking fruitlessly within sight of the harbor it had sailed from before it caught a good wind and was able to start its voyage.

The weather pattern we faced couldn't have been more challenging. A huge high-pressure system sat over northern Europe, and as a series of small lows moved across the Atlantic, they bounced off it and churned along its edge. That edge coincided with our course, so at best we had a strong adverse wind on our bow, and at worst we were fighting our way through the gales, one after another, that were generated as the lows collided with the high.

There was no extended period of favorable wind, only short stretches of a few hours each. Setting and dousing square sails over and over is a fatiguing job, and in the end it made more sense to simply travel under stays'ls and engine power.

With stormy seas, and without the steadying compressive effect of the square sails, conditions below deck were miserable most of the time.

But that's behind us now. We're in t-shirt weather-- soft, balmy, sub-tropical air-- and we are luxuriating in it.

DAY 14
Saturday, 1 March--Ashore in Funchal, Madeira

No travel agent could have planned it so well. Madeira was not even on our itinerary; it was a haven of convenience, an opportunity to regroup and heal our bruises. Yet our chance timing had brought us into port on the eve of carnival, and celebration was the order of the day.

"You can stay on the ship or go ashore," Captain McCarthy.

told the crew. "Just report back at 0800 Monday." That was all most of us needed. Freedom from stormy seas, freedom from crew duties, freedom from the confines of the ship itself-- this was heady stuff. People took off in all directions.

Only hours after our arrival yesterday, the festival kicked off with a giant city-wide costume party. Thousands of people of all ages-- couples, families with children, club groups-- promenad-ed, showing off their often spectacular costumes.

Mel, Pat and I decided there was nothing more desirable than a couple of nights in a stationary bed on an unmoving floor. We found an apartment with three beds in an apartment hotel and rented it for the weekend.

Today there were chores-- shopping for small items missed on the ship, like cuticle scissors (mine had been confiscated by airport security on my way to Ireland) and the obligatory hours-long session in an internet cafe. I may be moderately computer-literate but I have little patience with the protocols, and when the directions are all in Portuguese, I'm really confounded.

If Friday night was hectic, Saturday night was chaotic-- with color, sound, lights and movement. First came the fireworks, then the carnival parade, a three-hour spectacle. Dozens of bands, some hundreds-strong, marched through streets whose trees were bedecked with thousands of little lights. Each band's costumes, music and choreographed routines were distinctive and stunningly effective.

Our fellow crew members were glimpsed here and there, drifting through the densely packed crowds or drinking with seeming abandon at the sidewalk cafes. It was obvious that at the moment they had not a care for the ship, for the Captain-- or for the rest of the voyage, for that matter.

DAY 15
Sunday, 2 March-- Ashore in Funchal, Madeira

A*s* I stretched out in bed, luxuriating, I could think only of Rupert Brooke's poem, "The Great Lover," especially these lines: "These I have loved. . .the cool kindliness of sheets, that soon smooth away troubles, and the rough male kiss of blankets." There's nothing like 12 days on a small bobbing ship in large stormy seas to make one appreciate the soft, the gentle and the ordinary.

After a surfeit of sleep, it was time to explore this storied island. Madeira, I knew from reading nautical lore, was a crossroads for ships even 200 years ago, and that early familiarity brought wealthy British and European tourists to bask in its delightful climate.

Madeira is old luxury amid spectacular mountainous geography-- grand hotels, orange-tile-roofed houses undulating up and down valleys, banana plantations clinging to terraced hillsides.

To show us these delights, we engaged Peter (a corruption of his surname, Pita), an English-speaking taxi driver, who gave us a half-day's tour from Funchal up into the hills and out along the southern coast.

Peter took us by tortuous switchback roads to the highest point, where we gazed down at distant Funchal. He pointed out numerous springs of fresh, pure water, where we filled our water bottles (Madeirans carry containers in their cars and fill up whenever they pass one) and the levadas, 15th century irrigation sluices that run for hundreds of miles around the island. The paths that border them are a hiker's dream come true.

The mountain scenery was little short of fantastic, and the most distant point on our tour, isolated Nuns' Valley, was the most singular of all. In the bad old days of pirate raids, men who had been at sea for months came ashore wanting women,

167

and the nuns were their favorite targets because they were likely to be clean and disease-free. The nuns finally caught on, and when the raid alarm was sounded they fled to this remote valley.

A flicker of concern went through our minds as we thought of our own fellow sailors, but these are different times and they are certainly not pirates.

DAY 16
Monday, 3 March. Position at 0900: 32-31 N, 16-58 W

Just as we cast off about 0900, Roseanne from Cork screamed, "There's my friend on the dock; she has a gift basket for me." Too late, we were already underway. But a call from the pilot to the pilot boat effected a quick pickup, and when the boat returned to pick up the pilot, the basket was handed over.

All our crew are back aboard; none deserted or was shanghaied on another ship. The younger ones likely didn't have as much sleep as we did, but they did their own thing.

There was only one untoward incident. One of the young sail trainees couldn't hold his liquor; he came back to the ship early Sunday morning and stood bellowing like a bull in the mess deck, waking all hands. That led the Captain to impose a midnight curfew on Sunday and ban liquor being brought aboard.

As Madeira fades into the distance, we wish there had been more time to absorb its unique charms. It would have been fun to enjoy the classic Reid's Hotel, where Winston Churchill and George Bernard Shaw were once regulars, and to spend more time strolling along the Esplanade and dining in its fashionable restaurants. But what we saw was splendid, and we did manage to sample one of Madeira's timeless specialties-- its wine. Madeiran wine has been famous for so long that a glass of it sealed the signing of the American Declaration of

Independence, and George Washington had a pint with his dinner every night.

Now we are heading south, with all sails up, not a huge wind but doing somewhat less than three knots under sail alone. This is what we have all been waiting for.

DAY 17
Tuesday, 4 March. Position at 1400: 31-35 N, 17-04 W

A slow ship is a relaxing ship if you're not in a hurry to reach a destination, and we're not.

Top speed in the past 24 hours has been 2.4 knots, so at 0900 Madeira is only 55 to 60 nautical miles behind us; the lights were still visible early this morning. But we have time. The wind will freshen later today, and with that boost we expect to reach Santa Cruz, Tenerife, about 1000 Thursday, two days ahead of schedule.

As if someone had planned this voyage to be a saga of Saturnalia, Tenerife's carnival-- the biggest next to Rio-- will kick off the night we arrive, and we'll be docked right in the middle of it.

Meanwhile, ship's routines continue. A practice alarm brought us on deck, where Dr. Tom McCormack gave a first aid lecture; an "injured" person was carried up by litter from the bowels of the ship; we practiced getting into the yellow horseshoe with which a helicopter would haul us aloft if necessary; and fire hoses were unreeled and deployed while two crew members donned aluminum fire-fighting suits.

First officer Rob Matthews, who is also safety officer, tells us that our response time when the alarm sounds is getting better, but it's still subject to improvement.

Evidence of the ship's concern for safety is everywhere, and it is most impressive. If there is any inconvenience to rushing onto deck with our life jackets, wriggling into immersion suits

169

or going through a fire drill, we have only to remember that it is all for us and our safety, and that makes it more than acceptable.

DAY 18
Wednesday, 5 March. Position at 1030: 30-37 N, 16-37 W

A small bird flew aboard yesterday afternoon and perched, exhausted, on a rail atop the forward deckhouse. It has a brown-reddish breast but no one could identify it. After refueling on bread and water, it surveyed the ship and cannily decided to roost in the Captain's cabin. We hope it will find relatives in Tenerife.

In a deck lecture, the Captain observed that we are making our way south through Macronesia, the collective name the ancient Greeks gave to all these eastern Atlantic islands-- the Azores, Madeira, Canaries, Cape Verdes-- islands that in ancient times were the westernmost edge of the known world.

Ptolemy wrote of an island in the Atlantic called Erythria, the "Red Island," because of the dye it produced, and centuries later Madeira would still be famous for its "Dragon's Blood" resin. Early Christians believed it was a holy island that would disappear in the fog when sinners came near, and still later Madeira was thought to be part of the lost continent of Atlantis.

The Captain next turned his attention to tacking and wearing and illustrated with blackboard diagrams how the maneuvers are done. Then the crew fanned out and we practiced tacking (changing direction by going across the wind). A square-rigger can tack only in moderate winds. Too little wind and it would lose headway; too much and its back-winded sails would put an undue strain on the forestays.

The alternative to tacking is wearing, or falling off the wind and turning the ship to its new heading with the wind behind it ("jibing" to small boat sailors). Wearing ship in a slight wind, as we did, seems to take forever and the ship can lose a mile or two in the process.

It was a fine evening when we finished all that, so Sarah Caffery, our cook, had our food brought out to the foredeck and we dined picnic-style.

The engines powered us during the night but now we're under sail and doing a bit over 2 knots. By midday today, there was a 16-knot wind on our port beam, and we were making between 4 and 4.5 knots. A set of square sails filled with wind is a beautiful sight.

DAY 19

Thursday, 6 March. Position at 1400: 28-47 N, 16-10 W

For several glorious hours late yesterday, the ship was the star, and she seemed to know she was on stage. The wind was aft of our port beam and strengthening-- 14, 17, 19, up to 25. As the wind came up, so did our speed-- 4.5, 5.2, 5.7, 6.4 knots.

The full, rounded wind-packed sails were like rigid carved ivory, and they were driving, driving. You could almost feel the solid power moving from sails to masts to hull. Bosun Tom Harding and the watch leaders ran about making adjustments, and the one last sail in our inventory-- the spanker topsail-- was finally set. Then we all just stood and watched.

There's been plenty of time now to observe the ship's permanent company in action, and I have only the highest praise for all of them.

Captain Tom McCarthy is an experienced master. He sailed *Asgard*, the Irish sail training ship, to Australia. No remote figure, he frequently joins us at the crew mess table and is a fount of information.

Rob Matthews, the first mate and safety officer, is committed to our welfare and goes out of his way to be helpful. Thanks to Rob, the ship is clean and orderly. Rowan MacSweeney, second mate and communications officer, is my key to sending these transmissions. He sets up the telex in the wheelhouse and I balance its little keyboard on my knees and type out my messages.

Martin (Tash) Treacy, third mate, is a Macintosh computer user, as I am, and he's given me many helpful hints for dealing with the ship's computer. Peter O'Regan, the engineer, is everywhere at once, putting his ear to the heartbeat of the engines and generators, monitoring the water maker and the sewage treatment plant, keeping the heads operating smoothly.

Tom Harding is the perfect bosun-- not only the consummate master of the rigging but a great story teller as well. Dave Nolan, bosun's mate, is a man of all skills-- carpenter, machinist, toolmaker, and improviser. Along with Mark Tighe, Boyce Nolan and Frida Bjorsell, the watch leaders, these people are the vital core of the ship.

Having seen them perform through the worst we've encountered, I'm more than content to put my life in their hands for the rest of the voyage. I hope they will be treated royally, as they deserve, by every American they meet.

DAY 20
Friday, 7 March-- Ashore in Santa Cruz, Tenerife

Santa Cruz, administrative center of the western Canary Islands, is one of the busiest ports in Spain and one of the deepest in the world (The islands are really volcanic mountains that drop off sharply into the ocean depths). As the pilot guided us slowly into the huge harbor yesterday, we were amazed at the array of container ships, cruise liners, inter-island hydrofoils and ferries. The *Jeanie Johnston* was the smallest, and certainly the most distinctive, of all the vessels in view.

Rising behind the city are the Anaga Mountains, and far back beyond them is Mt. Teide. At almost 12,500 feet, it is the highest peak in Spain and the highest elevation anywhere in the Atlantic Ocean. Teide's last great eruption was in 1492, and Columbus observed it from the nearby island of Gomera just before he left on his first voyage of discovery.

There will be some changing of the guard in Santa Cruz. Our 15 young Irish sail trainees and their leader will leave, to be replaced by a new group for the Atlantic crossing. Some of our other voyage crew members will depart, too, but all are staying for a few days to enjoy Carnival.

Tenerife's frantic festival runs from February 26 to March 9, the first Sunday in Lent, and we're here in time for its blockbuster culmination.

Sleeping in a real bed in Madeira was so delicious that many want to repeat the experience. Several of us have put up at the Anaga Hotel, a few blocks from the ship and close to the heart of downtown. Pat McGrath, Jim O'Brien and I are sharing a room, and after getting settled we explore the carnival scene.

This year's carnival theme is The Far East, and in the Piazza de Espana, at the foot of the Calle del Castillo, a pedestrian mall that is the heart of tourist downtown, the Santa Cruzans have built an immense stage set. Complete with ornate towers that have a Malaysian look about them, it serves as the backdrop for one Spanish rock band after another, from dusk till God knows when. Nearby streets are decorated with thousands of red balloons and small faery lights hung in the trees overhead.

We stop for a beer at a sidewalk cafe and watch the crowd go by. At a table nearby a human-sized Miss Piggy in a farmerette costume sits rocking to the beat of the music. Other costumed oddities float slowly by.

Some fellow crew members drift into view, and there is much loud greeting and boisterous back-slapping. It makes us realize how close we have become over recent days. Amid strangers in a strange country, we are genuinely glad to see one another.

DAY 21
Saturday, 8 March-- Ashore in Santa Cruz, Tenerife

We have found an internet cafe, and the directions are now in Spanish rather than Portuguese, but they are just as confusing. Fortunately one of the attendants speaks English, and suddenly all the frustrations are relieved by just a few simple hints. Piled-up email messages have been read, and we have communicated with home and friends.

Our companions have scattered in all directions-- some to shop, others to meet friends or relatives who are on Tenerife. And at least once a day most of us touch base with the ship to see what's going on and, I suspect, for a secret reassurance that it is still there and hasn't left without us.

The ship has been turned inside out, and much of what it carried now lies on the dock. The young sail trainees-- 15 of them plus their supervisor-- sit disconsolately on their luggage, waiting to leave for home. A new group for the second, longer, leg of the voyage will soon replace them.

Everything below decks has been scrubbed to within an inch of its life, every bunk has been stripped, and the 40 mattresses are airing on the dock. But they are not idle. The young crewmembers have bunched them into one huge mat, and they are competing with somersaults and other acrobatic turns.

Bosun's mate Dave Nolan is a born monkey (He has often been seen swinging from the shrouds or, with a handy rope, leaping to the dock before the gangway is in place, like Tarzan on a vine). But he is no match for watch leader Frida Bjorsell, who has represented her native Sweden internationally in the sport of acrobatics. We watch in awe as she does a series of back flips.

This is the last big night of carnival, and perhaps for that reason the music seems to be blaring even louder. To protect our eardrums, we have sought refuge in a restaurant a few

174

blocks from downtown. Paul Dolan's wife has joined him, and several of us have dinner together. We talk of the voyage, recounting stories of the ship's rock-and-roll behavior and laughing uproariously at some of the strange predicaments we found ourselves in. Even the cramped quarters and seasickness become subjects of merriment now that we are on solid ground.

DAY 22
Sunday, 9 March-- Ashore in Santa Cruz, Tenerife

It's Sunday morning, and up the slippery pavement of Calle del Castello the wrack of carnival is everywhere. Last night was the crux, the end-all of celebration, and this morning it shows. The street cleaners have done their washing but the garbage collectors have not yet arrived. Thousands of bottles and cans and all the other detritus of carnival await them.

The celebrants are still here but they are walking zombies, padding about with no destination, wound up from the night before, on the move all night and still going. We heard them in our uneasy sleep, and closing the hotel windows didn't shut out the ear-shattering music to which they were moving.

Now we walk among them-- clowns, oriental potentates, furry animals, knights on horseback, Miss Piggy and her friends still going strong. I stop on a street corner to consult my city map, and there is a tap on my shoulder. A 6-foot-3 man dressed as a woman stops to help. He has a huge blond wig and an alcoholic breath, but his smile is pleasant and he is fuzzily sober. I thank him and he walks away, his purple dress swishing.

Cross-dressing is a prime feature of Tenerife's carnival, and you're never sure which gender you are seeing, though there are some clues. When the women are overtall and teetering perilously on their high heels, that's one. When the men sport exaggerated mustaches and bushy black eyebrows, that's another.

Further along the street, three people in orange wigs are coaxing life into an ancient Volkswagen bug that is smeared with orange paint. In the street near them, a human effigy lies burning. "George W. Bush!" shouts a young woman, pointing to it. We strike up a conversation with her and her companions. They are not radicals, just wholesome young Spaniards, and it soon is apparent they like Americans but are turned off by the idea of war. We tell them about our ship, and, computer-savvy all, they want web addresses where they can follow the voyage.

Going aboard the ship now evokes mixed emotions. It's always a thrill to see and we still love it, but it was the scene of many discomforts. After three days in our hotel, the floors are no longer tilting, and the beds remain stationary all night. The feeling is strange but welcome.

We will sail on Friday, 14 March, a change from the original sailing date, the 13th. "Is there some seafaring superstition involved here?" I asked Rob Matthews. "No sailor likes to sail on the 13th," he said with an enigmatic smile.

DAY 23
Monday, 10 March-- Ashore in Santa Cruz, Tenerife

The celebrants have gone home and the clean-up crews are at work. For the next several days the public squares will be filled with noise of a different sort as scores of workmen begin the task of disassembling all the elaborate carnival structures-- the ornamental gates and pagodas and the huge sound stage itself.

The one carnival event I wish I'd seen took place before we arrived. It's called The Burial of the Sardine and sounds totally bizarre. The sardine, an enormous structure of wood and cloth, is pulled through the streets in a very irreverent parade. Preceding it are some 200 men dressed as popes, nuns and priests. Some of them carry huge dildos with which they bless

176

the crowd, while others carry giant books that-- with pious express-ions-- they open to show onlookers a selection of pornographic pictures. Following the sardine are hundreds of mourners, widows all in black, but not the kind of mourning garb you'd expect. Picture instead black stockings, suspenders and thigh-high black boots.

This wild outbreak, social observers note, has something to do with the years during which carnival was repressed when General Franco ruled Spain. When he died in 1975, carnival came back more exotic and erotic than it had ever been.

While we putter and enjoy ourselves, the ship's permanent crew have had little time to relax. Every day now is busy, preparing the ship for its nearly-4,000-mile voyage to Florida. The fuel tanks have been cleaned and refilled. All the rigging has been checked and repairs made where necessary, and the standing rigging-- the shrouds and stays that support the masts-- has been retuned.

Taking aboard food for 40 people for 40 days has been a major task. The most challenging job, says the Captain, has been finding space in which to stow it. In the weeks to come, we will be amazed to see the galley crew retrieving stores from the most unlikely places under floors and behind bulkheads.

The new rescue boat has been delivered and on one of our visits to the ship we saw Tom and Dave and Rob assembling its accessories and preparing to swing it aboard.

All the ship needs now is crew, but the new sail trainees don't report until 13 March, and the rest of us are still on the town.

DAY 24
Tuesday, 11 March-- Ashore in Santa Cruz, Tenerife

Puerto de la Cruz, on the north side of the island, is

Tenerife's most visited city, and Pat McGrath, Jim O'Brien and I decided to join the visitors' ranks. The easiest way was by bus, and the ride was only 40 minutes or so. For most of the way, the distant view was dominated by snow-dusted Mt. Teide.

While Santa Cruz is insulated from the sea by its extensive docks and warehouses, Puerto de la Cruz is spectacularly sited directly on the water. All its narrow streets run to the sea, and the heart of its charm is the sea front itself, with its overlook sites, promenades and pedestrian malls. The view, from a slight elevation, is of crashing surf on a jumbled rocky shore.

The thousands of tourists who spend their holidays here know a nirvana when they see one. The Canaries, just four degrees from the Tropic of Cancer and close to the African coast, have a subtropical climate whose temperatures vary between 64.4 and 75.2 degrees Fahrenheit all year round. Combine eternal springtime with visual splendor and the result is Puerto de la Cruz.

The Canaries were known in antiquity, and they had many names. Homer, in the 9th century BC, wrote of the Elysian Fields, where "men live peacefully without suffering snow, hard winters or rain, enjoying perenially cool air." Herodotus, in the 5th century BC, referred to them as The Fortunate Islands, and other early historians called them The Hesperides.

Pat McGrath, from northern Ireland, who is leaving us after completing the Fenit-Tenerife voyage, wants to stay here for a week or so if he can find a place. Pat has been in Tenerife before, and now that the ship has left him here, he is eager to extend this stay. We can understand why.

Other members of our Irish crew, too, are starting to make disparaging comparisons between their home climate and that of the Canaries.

If I were Captain McCarthy, I might worry just a little about subjecting my crew members to such temptations.

178

DAY 25
Wednesday, 12 March-- Ashore in Santa Cruz, Tenerife

I am sitting in a sidewalk cafe near the waterfront in Santa Cruz, lingering over coffee and a bun. Carnival is over, and the huge sound stage across the plaza that was its focus is being dismantled. Drifting out of the cafe behind me is the unmistakably plaintive tone of Louis Armstrong's trumpet playing "I Found My Thrill On Blueberry Hill."

It makes me think of all the cultural influences that impact an international crossroads like this. American jazz is only one. The carnival bands that played here recently reflected a dazzling assortment of musical backgrounds-- African, Spanish, Cuban and Italian among them.

On the *Jeanie Johnston*, too, we have our cultural diversity. My best count comes up with about 24 Republican Irish, 11 Northern Irish, one Englishman, two Americans and one Swede among the permanent crew and the voyage crew.

But that doesn't tell it all. We have a variety of religious and political viewpoints. The Northern Irish are equally split between Catholic and Protestant, a cultural divide that in their locale often seems as deep and impassable as that between Israelis and Palestinians.

Why do we all get on so well together? Because we are thrown together in a common cause-- to get the ship to America and to ensure the success of her voyage. In that sense we all know we are a part of something bigger than ourselves, and it cancels out our differences.

My late friend, author and columnist Dick Kleiner, once wrote, "I think our earth will eventually have a One World society-- one language, one people, one religion. That is the only way in which we will be able to make it. The petty

179

squabbles we now have, based on religion and race and territorial imperatives, will have to cease or our planet is doomed. And being an optimist, I think our planet will survive and flourish."

The fulfillment of Dick's vision is a long way off, but, as we're proving on the *Jeanie Johnston*, we can all work toward it by thinking and acting as citizens of the world rather than as Irish, Germans, Americans, Presbyterians, Catholics, Jews, Muslims or whatever other national or religious tags we bear.

DAY 26
Thursday, 13 March-- Ashore in Santa Cruz, Tenerife

Captain McCarthy has decided that since we are crossing the Atlantic at about the same latitude Columbus did in 1492, we should try to follow, and in effect memorialize, his voyage. Columbus's last stop in the Canaries was the island of Gomera, where he took on fresh water and prayed in the local church for fair winds and a safe passage.

When we up anchor tomorrow, we will head for the port of San Sebastian on Gomera, and the plan is to spend several hours there, departing late in the afternoon. We will have a chance to see the church and say some prayers of our own.

We will then set sail, as Columbus did, and follow his 500-year-old wake to San Salvador, his New World landfall. From there, it will be just a short hop to West Palm Beach, our transatlantic destination and the first stop on the *Jeanie Johnston*'s summer port tour of the East Coast.

By luck, I have brought with me a copy of Columbus's journal, and I will try to track our daily progress against his. The journal cites distance sailed in leagues, and a careful reading makes clear that a league was four miles, but I will have to search further to learn whether or not these are nautical miles.

Columbus's plan was simple. He would avoid the huge seas

180

and strong head winds of the North Atlantic, run south before the northerlies off Spain and North Africa and then take a right turn at the Canary Islands. He knew from local voyages that the winter winds in the Canaries blew from the east; he also knew that the latitude of the Canaries was roughly the same as that of Japan, and from Japan he would make his way to the Indies.

Little did he know that between the Canaries and Japan lay something new, immense and fantastic that would change the shape of the world forever.

As the three caravels approached the Canaries, the Pinta's rudder jumped out of gear. Columbus continued to Gomera, took on water and food supplies, then returned with his other captains to Tenerife, where they repaired the Pinta. They then sailed back to Gomera and anchored off San Sebastian.

Before the three little ships turned west into the great unknown, two singular events took place. Columbus met and, according to a shipmate, fell in love with a beautiful lady, the widow of the former governor of the island; and they "saw a great fire coming from the mountain of the island of Tenerife, which is remarkably lofty." It was a dramatic start for a voyage whose ending was to change the course of history.

DAY 27
Friday, 14 March-- Underway, Tenerife to Gomera

I am standing on the afterdeck in the moonlight, watching the fading lights of Tenerife glimmer in our wake when suddenly I am transported back in time.

It's April 1943, and I stand at the taffrail of the British troop ship *Andes,* outbound from Newport News to Casablanca with 15,000 American soldiers aboard. By chance or by fate, I am found to be the senior 2nd Lieutenant aboard, so I am put in charge of the guard unit.

One of our principal jobs is to ensure total blackout conditions at night. Even the flick of a cigarette lighter on deck might be seen several miles away by an alert U-boat commander. Security is crucial since the *Andes* travels alone and has no escort to protect her.

Fifteen thousand lives are a huge responsibility for a 22-year-old, and I take to sleeping during the day and prowling the ship at night. Once I catch a major about to light up. When he understands what is at stake, he is cooperative and goes back inside.

I spend a lot of time watching the stars, and I become aware that our course is constantly changing. Communication between us, the passengers, and the ship's company is forbidden, but in the course of my nighttime prowlings, I come close to an off-limits area and one night I strike up an acquaintance with a young ship's officer who is on watch. He tells me the Admiralty has determined that it takes a U-boat eight-and-a-half minutes to access a target, launch a torpedo and score a hit, so the *Andes* is changing course every seven-and-a-half minutes. We are zigzagging across the Atlantic.

He tells me also that the *Andes* is well known to the German wolf packs and much sought after because the lucky U-boat skipper who bagged her would surely be a candidate for the coveted Iron Cross.

We go through two great Atlantic storms, and down below, where the bunks are 10-high and the men sleep in shifts, the decks are slippery with vomit. Most, like me, have never been on a ship before. After each storm, 5,000 men are allowed on deck at a time while clean-up proceeds below. Crap shoots and card games break out, and jokes fly back and forth between farmers and city kids about who threw up the most last night.

We arrive in Casablanca on a foggy morning, and as we creep past the harbor buoys, we see bodies and debris floating past. My friend the ship's officer tells me that German Intelligence has learned the *Andes'* schedule, and U-boats were lying in wait but they mistakenly torpedoed the ship just ahead of us.

Back aboard the *Jeanie Johnston*, I wonder idly why the *Andes* left a brilliant phosphorescent wake while we do not. Then I realize that her huge propellers were churning up tons of seawater while we glide silently along under wind power alone.

There's another difference, and it's one to cherish-- we don't have any U-boats chasing us. The seas at least are at peace these days.

DAY 28

Saturday, 15 March. Position at 1700: 27-59 N, 17-15 W

Through the night, a fine northeast trade wind moved us from Tenerife to Gomera, where we docked about 1130 this morning at the port of San Sebastian.

The church where Columbus prayed is ancient-looking but well cared for, and most of us spent some time there, each immersed in his own prayer or meditation. But then a funeral moved in and there was no opportunity to see or do anything more. We had learned upon landing that Columbus lived here on Gomera for a while, and his house is still preserved, but unfortunately it was not open today.

Like many of the earth's out-of-the-way places, this one has its share of escapees who have had a change of heart. "Please help us to buy a ticket home," said a roughly lettered sign behind a display of handcrafted jewelry in San Sebastian's market. The youthful proprietors had a tired look about them.

Jim Callery and I roamed the market together. Jim was intent on buying a bottle of the Canaries' finest wine, and he finally found it. We couldn't read the label, but it was, the seller assured Jim, the very best brand on the islands. Later, at the tourist information center, he showed it to the woman in charge and she laughed. "You've bought a bottle of honey," she said. "I thought it felt heavy," Jim admitted.

We have a new contingent of young sail trainees and paying crew members aboard now, and we are in process of getting acquainted. The oldest appear to be Tom and Maura Cannon, from the Dublin area-- the first and only married couple on the voyage. Tom is 74 and an active sailor.

As we left San Sebastian at 1530, I glanced at the distant horizon and noticed that Tenerife's volcano was not erupting. We would have a less spectacular sendoff than Columbus.

DAY 29
Sunday, 16 March. Position at 1400: 26-45 N, 19-08 W

Wind is what sailing is all about, but wind can be a mixed blessing. At the outset of this voyage, we had too much, and from the wrong direction. Too little is almost as bad, but we are now entering that part of the Atlantic that for centuries has been every sailor's happy medium-- the trade wind belt.

Captain McCarthy has given us a tutorial on the trades. They were so named because their reliability permitted trading ships to carry on regular commerce, and their location has long been established. They are air streams that blow along the eastern and southern flanks of the great mid-Atlantic system known as the Bermuda-Azores High, and because the peripheral winds of a high pressure system in the northern hemisphere always blow clockwise, they blow from the northeast or east-- right across the Atlantic to the Caribbean.

The trades start blowing seriously between 25 and 30 degrees north latitude, and the farther south you go the stronger they blow. The Captain's plan is to steer southwest and go down to 20 degrees latitude to find stronger winds. We need them because we have almost 3,400 miles to go and will have to make better than an average five knots to get to Florida by 16 April.

We are now on the track of Columbus, though it will be

difficult to make comparisons until we have had a few full days of sailing. Columbus at the moment is at a disadvantage. The trade wind failed us at the outset from Gomera, as it did him, but we motored through the night and are only now sailing, whereas Columbus was becalmed for three days.

He may yet catch up to us, though, because of the speed of his ships. Caravels of his day often made up to nine-and-a-half knots in a strong wind, and could sometimes do 12 knots. For five consecutive days, Columbus averaged 142 miles per day and on his best day's run he averaged eight knots. The *Jeanie Johnston*'s hull speed is about 10 knots and the best speed she has made-- in a gale in the Irish Sea-- was close to nine-and-a-half.

As naval historian Samuel Eliot Morison points out, improvements in sailing vessels since 1492 have been more in comfort than in speed. Square riggers of around 1500, he notes, could sail closer to the wind than those of 1900 because they had less standing rigging to prevent the yards being braced back sharply.

DAY 30
Monday, 17 March. Position at 1430: 25-39 N, 20-52 W

St. Patrick's Day on an Irish ship can only be a special occasion, and this one is. It began this morning with spirited music on deck.

Among the new sail trainees is one with a strong voice, a good hand with the guitar and a store of Irish ballads. He was accompanied by more beating of large and small drums, pots and pans and flutes and pipes than I've ever seen or heard at one time.

St. Patrick has given us a favorable wind for the second day, for which we are all grateful, and it appears that a full moon will rise tonight in the good Saint's honor.

As if all these good signs weren't enough, just as the music was reaching its crescendo a pigeon circled the ship three or four times and came to roost on the rescue boat.

The crew immediately christened the bird Paddy O'Pigeon. It's a professional pigeon with a band on one leg, but what its mission is we can only guess. Homing pigeons supposedly have a range of several hundred miles. We are more than 200 miles from the Canaries now, and as the pigeon rests, we move still farther away. We hope the bird has a plan in mind, though if it wants to see West Palm Beach it is welcome to stay.

An al fresco lunch and more music followed the pigeon's arrival. Tables and benches have been brought on deck, and if the good weather continues, lunch-- and perhaps dinner-- will be served under the sky.

Tom Harding, Dave Nolan and watch leaders Mark Tighe and Boyce Nolan are stitching two sets of stuns'ls (studdingsails) and making the yards that will support them. They'll be mounted on the mainmast and foremast outboard of the topsails and topgallants and should give us a bit more speed.

As for Columbus, it's too early to make comparisons, but at least I know now what we have to work with. Columbus recorded his distances sailed in leagues, and his league equaled four Roman miles (4,850 feet). A league of that length translates into about 3.19 nautical miles.

DAY 31
Tuesday, 18 March. Position at 1400: 24-53 N, 22-28 W

We're at the halfway point of this voyage-- 30 days behind us and 30 ahead. Since our second day out of Gomera, we've had the northeast trade winds behind us-- no engines, quiet nights, steady ship, full sails, and delightful weather-- the best a wooden ship can offer.

I'll say this about wooden ships: once you've learned to love them, they can do no wrong. It's the romance and the sense of history that have drawn us to this tiny moving speck in the Atlantic, and the blemishes we can put up with.

"What about the water that drips down on my bunk when they hose the deck?" I asked engineering officer Peter O'Regan. "Don't worry about it," said Peter. "When we get closer to the tropics, and the seams open a bit, it'll get even worse."

Even so, Peter and bosun's mate Dave Nolan have rigged a sheet of plastic to divert the water away from my bunk, and tomorrow they will caulk the deck above my head. Peter is philosophic about this. "Wooden ships leak," he says. "That's their way. As long as we keep most of the water out, we're all right."

After they left, I discovered that the plastic did indeed channel the dripping water away from my bunk. It now went onto Jim's bunk. I couldn't conceal this fact from Jim. We laughed and took the plastic sheet down.

On the run from Fenit to Madeira, water dripped down my neck at the mess table, and I saw water sloshing across the floor from someone's compartment. There are other small annoyances. Jim stowed some belongings in a convenient niche next to his bunk only to hear them splash into the bilge far below.

On a cruise ship, we'd be suing. Here we pay for the privilege of being uncomfortable.

But all that is forgotten when I step on deck at night and see a startlingly brilliant moon illuminating the sails with a ghostly daylight; Orion's Belt sparkling like diamonds over the top of the foremast; soft, bright cumulus clouds ringing the horizon; a pleasant 17-knot wind moving us at five to six knots; and a gentle sea with long slow swells that add just enough motion to keep us alert when moving about. How could life be any sweeter?

DAY 32
Wednesday, 19 March. Position at 1500: 23-01 N, 24-30 W

At 0200 today we entered a new time zone, so clocks went back an hour. We're now only four time zones from the US east coast. The Captain had planned to go down to 22 degrees latitude, but the winds are so good here (17-20 knots) he's decided to continue for now as we are.

Paddy O'Pigeon has taken off on a reconnaissance mission to the west. In the direction he's heading, it's something over 3,000 miles as the pigeon flies to West Palm Beach. We hope he'll give up his quest and come back to roost.

The mysteries of a wooden ship continue to reveal themselves. Sitting in the great cabin with a fair wind moving us, I heard serious groaning from the mizzen mast, which goes right through the cabin to the keel below. A close look revealed a vertical crack in the mast. As the mast flexed, the crack opened and closed. I ran to find bosun Tom Harding. "In the first place," said Tom, "it's not a crack. If it goes with the grain it's a 'shake," and it's nothing to be greatly concerned about. It might go on for months or even years before it becomes a real problem." Still, I hate to hear it groan.

Yesterday saw another general alarm practice drill. A simulated fire was extinguished and a simulated injured person was carried up from below on a stretcher.

After lunch, a haircut marathon got underway on deck. Dave Nolan was the first victim, and he emerged with a fierce-looking Mohican, or Mohawk, haircut. Others got the same-- even watch leader Frida Bjorsell, and Tom Harding and the Captain joined in the fun. Watch leader John Judge ended up with a set of long ringlets that the girls offered to braid, but he wisely turned down the offer.

The reason for this madness, I learned, is that we have crossed the Tropic of Cancer, the parallel of latitude that marks

188

the northern boundary of the so-called Torrid Zone, or tropics. I had thought only crossing the Equator sparked such behavior.

I started a beard some days ago but gave it up after looking in the mirror. I may work instead on a seaman's ponytail. Rob Matthews, the first officer, sports a fine ponytail and has offered to advise me, though it may take a longer voyage than this one to do it right.

DAY 33
Thursday, 20 March. Noon position: 22-28 N. 25-07 W.
Distance from West Palm Beach: 3,028 miles

We now have the *Jeanie Johnston*'s official US port visiting schedule from her arrival in West Palm Beach on 17 April through her departure from New York on 14 July. We hope there will be a resounding welcome in each port.

Our present sailing mode is so different from that of the Fenit -to-Madeira leg of the voyage there might almost be two *Jeanie Johnstons.*

Since leaving the Canaries behind, each day has been a fine one. With the trade wind behind us and blowing at 17 to 20 knots much of the time now, we can easily do from five and a half knots to seven knots. That moves us at a rate of 130 to 160 miles per 24 hours.

We are heading generally west but can go a bit farther south, so that gives us a little maneuvering room. Depending on where the wind is, we can adjust our heading slightly to get it on either our port or starboard quarter, the best point of sailing for a square rigger.

Adjustments can also be made to the sails themselves-- bracing the yards back to port or starboard, or squaring them. If the wind were too strong, we'd need to reduce sail.

At the moment we have a little over 3,000 miles to go and 30 days in which to do it. If we did six knots constantly, we'd be in Florida in 20 days. A little over four knots, day in and day out, would get us there exactly on time.

But there's no certainty to the weather, the wind or the sea. That's why we must make good speeds while we can and get mileage in the bank, so to speak, against the possibility of bad weather, foul winds or periods of no wind that might lie ahead.

Meanwhile, the sailing is glorious-- all sails up most of the time, sunshine and t-shirt weather above decks, steadiness and quiet below. There's always a slight bit of rolling in the swells, but after our Fenit-Madeira run, it's like a garden party. Will we get tired of it and wish for some challenges again? Maybe, but at the moment we are more than content with what we have.

DAY 34

Friday, 21 March. Noon position: 21-34 N, 28-45 W. Distance from West Palm Beach: 2,887 miles

Watch leader Mark, trolling off our stern, yesterday caught a 16-pound dorado, and today Sarah served it up for lunch. Meanwhile, Tom Harding and his helpers are assembling the aluminum spars for the stuns'ls on the foredeck.

We are far from everything out here-- no newspapers, no television-- but BBC news is keeping us up to date with the war in Iraq, and we are of two minds about it.

Political viewpoints aside, each of us is torn between (1) curiosity and concern, and (2) annoyance that the world is intruding on our little idyll. One way we deal with our dilemma is through humor. There's no disrespect in this. We know the world has serious problems, but there's little we can do to solve them.

Humor helps us maintain our equilibrium and keeps us from making pontifical judgments based on very little information. As the only American aboard, I am the focus of much of this humor. "If America is at war," says Denis of Dublin, "and

Ireland remains neutral, it might be an embarrassment to have you on board." "Should I be clapped in irons?" I ask. "Quite possibly," says John Judge. "Where is the brig?" I ask, wondering if it might be a leak-free area. I shouldn't have asked. "The deep freeze would have to do," says John Gill. "It would keep you cool until we figured out what to do with you." "It would be simpler to pitch him overboard," says Denis.

Being the lone American on a ship full of Irishmen is an interesting experience. I like and enjoy them all, but frequently they'll get off on a line of conversation that leaves me wholly adrift. It'll be about some Irish politician, a famous Irish scandal or the history of some specific Irish location. Ireland is a small enough country so that everyone knows these things, but I am totally out of it.

Then there's the matter of dialects. The Dublin accent requires the least attention on my part. When it's Cork or Kerry, though, I must keep constantly on my toes, and even then I lose a third of it. Then there are those few to whom I just nod and smile without grasping a word said. But then it works both ways. I notice some who must strain to catch what my foreign accent is trying to tell them.

DAY 35

Saturday, 22 March. Noon position: 21-26 N, 30-51 W.
Distance to West Palm Beach: 2771 Miles.

It's been a week since we left Gomera, which was also Columbus's departure point for his first voyage of discovery. Comparing our progress with his on a day-to-day basis didn't make sense-- he was becalmed for the first three days while we simply motored our way to where the wind was-- but on a weekly basis, the figures may have more meaning.

Our track is roughly the same as his, and our occasional use of the engines will have less impact as we build up more sailing mileage. In the first week we made 894 miles while Columbus did 588 (Some of his daily progress is reported in Roman miles of 4,850 feet each and some in leagues of four Roman miles each; for our purpose, these have been converted into nautical miles).

Our best day's run was 178 miles and Columbus's was 182. Our worst mileage was 65 while his was zero. It took Columbus 36 days to sail from Gomera to San Salvador; our schedule calls for us to do the same in some 30 days.

If we continue to get winds that move us at speeds of at least five knots, we probably won't use engine power, so with each passing day and week, the comparison will be more valid. Even more fascinating than the figures are the observations in the Journal.

Unfortunately we don't have the original. When Columbus returned from the first voyage, he presented his logbook to the King and Queen. Some time later they gave him a copy, which was kept in the family archives. A Dominican historian, Las Casas, made an abstract of it, copying some parts word for word and abridging others, and his abstract is all we have today.

In it, the Admiral of the Ocean Sea notes on September 13 that the currents were against him, meaning probably that he was slightly to the north and west of us. Ocean currents are well charted today, and we have been aided by the Canary Current and will shortly enter the North Equatorial Current, which could give us a boost of up to one and a half knots.

Columbus describes "temperate breezes, so that it was a great delight to enjoy the mornings, and nothing was lacking except to hear nightingales." The weather, he said, "was like April in Andalusia." Some 500 years later, we are finding much the same.

DAY 36

Sunday, 23 March. Noon position: 21-29 N, 33-23 W.
Distance to West Palm Beach: 2,629.

The wind has let us down, dropping to less than 10 knots, and we have been under power all night and into this morning. We are near the bottom of that gentle curve the trade winds and currents follow in their perpetual clockwise motion around the great central Bermuda-Azores high. Our course, therefore, is approaching due west.

The sun rises almost directly behind us and drops, blazing and sizzling, into the sea off our bow. We shade our eyes as it sets and watch in vain for the green flash-- a tropical phenomenon that occurs occasionally when conditions are just right. I've seen it twice-- both times in Grenada. Rob, the first mate, has seen it once, but Capt. McCarthy, in 32 years at sea, has not been so lucky.

The North Equatorial Current is giving us a push of only about half a knot-- not enough to do much good against the wind deficit, so we must continue to motor. The Captain's rule of thumb is that if our speed drops below five knots for an appreciable period, he wants the engines on.

The plan is to arrive off San Salvador on April 11 or 12, anchor and go ashore by boat to touch base with Columbus, put in briefly at Nassau, and then head for West Palm Beach.

We have received a sobering telex message on the ship's EGC (Enhanced Group Calling) service, which gives us weather and other information via satellite. It's a safety message directed primarily to ships in the Persian Gulf area, and it warns that Coalition Naval Forces "are prepared to take measures in self-defense," and that "all maritime vessels or activities that are determined to be threats. . .will be subject to defensive measures, including boarding, seizure, disabling or destruction without regard to registry or location." Vessels operating in the war zone are "subject to query, being stopped, boarded and searched." If they are found to be carrying contraband, bound for Iraq, they are "subject to detention, seizure or destruction." This is serious business, and we are glad we are making our way placidly across the Atlantic, far from the war zone.

DAY 37
Monday, 24 March. Noon position: 21-31 N, 35-41 W.
Distance to West Palm Beach: 2,504.

One of the factors that moved me to make this voyage was a 16-year-old Irish girl. She sailed these seas to America 140 years ago and grew up to be my grandmother. I still don't know where in County Cork Joanna O'Brien was born, and I learned nothing more about her during my recent time in Ireland. But it was partly in her honor that I wanted to sail on the *Jeanie Johnston*, and one of my goals was to try to imagine how a sea voyage would have affected an Irish teenager in 1863.

We have Irish teenagers aboard, and I thought that would help, but it hasn't. These young people are educated, computer-literate and worldly-wise. They have traveled; they are familiar with American music, movies and popular culture. Some have American friends; most follow the news and have world political views.

The cultural chasm that separates them from 16-year-old Joanna O'Brien is unbridgeable and unfathomable. She was alone, illiterate, and without resources. Very likely a country girl with limited contacts, she was born in 1847, the worst famine year, and was lucky to have survived as an infant.

Why her family shipped her off to America is unknown to me. Was it the despair of poverty, the hope of opportunity, or both, that motivated them? She arrived in a New York whose employment ads invariably ended with the phrase, "Irish need not apply." The two Irish cultural classifications of those days were "lace curtain" and "shanty," and Joanna was as deep into

194

the "shanty" category as she could be.

But she made her way to New Jersey, found a job as a house maid with a well-to-do family and married the family's Scottish gardener. That much I know, but how she felt about, and reacted to, her ocean voyage will remain a mystery to me.

DAY 38
Tuesday, 25 March. Noon position: 21-44 N, 38-04 W.
Distance to West Palm Beach: 2,375.

The wind was slowly dying, and if it quit altogether, the Captain promised us a swimming stop out here in the middle of the Atlantic. He'd be able to do that only if it were totally calm. Then we'd douse the sails, heave to, and the ship would sit motionless in the water.

But just as all hands were looking forward to a dip, tell-tale ripples on the water told us a wind was approaching from the northeast, so plans were changed. All sails were set and we began moving again. Making headway is more important than anything.

Meanwhile, we were slowly getting the ship ready for her premiere appearance in America. Over several days, we sanded and oiled the rails all the way around from bow to stern, and now they are being varnished.

Next came the belaying pins, which, dropped into holes in the pin rails and pipe rails, hold the scores of sheets, lines and halyards that control the sails. There must be more than 100 of them in use, and we removed as many as we could at a time, then sanded, oiled and varnished them.

These communal work sessions are highly social events, usually interrupted by a rest break, with coffee, tea, fruit and cookies brought out from the galley. This morning we embarked on the most ambitious task yet-- sanding, oiling and varnishing the entire forward deck house. This will take several days, and then we must tackle the aft deck house.

There comes a point in any long voyage when boredom spawns either mutiny or silliness, and silliness seems to be creeping in on us-- only among the young, of course.

Outrageous hair styles have already run their course. Now novel face makeup is in order, and cross-dressing. We hear giggles from a secluded area of the foredeck, and there is our watch leader, John, in a girl's dress, wearing makeup and posing for photos with several of the real girls.

It's something we wouldn't have expected from John, who is taking this voyage as a break from his pursuit of a PhD in computer sciences. But life at sea changes people. I wonder who will be next.

DAY 39
Wednesday, 26 March. Noon position: 20-49 N, 40-28 W.
Distance to West Palm Beach: 2,250 miles.

In a deck talk today, the Captain said he hoped he wouldn't have to go any farther south, and would do so only if necessary to catch the wind. We left the Canaries at the right time, he said, because they had three days of adverse wind from the southeast following our departure.

A ship passed us on the starboard side today; the Captain said she was bound from the Orinoco to Lisbon, possibly with a cargo of lumber.

Since leaving the Canaries, we have been navigating the old-fashioned way-- by the sun and the stars. John Gill, alternate second mate, has had more than 50 years at sea, 30 of them on square-rigged ships, and several of us have been trying, with his help, to absorb the principles of celestial navigation. John brought his sextant, which had been gathering dust for more than 20 years, and began taking noon sightings of the sun to determine latitude.

"This is the easy stuff," said John. All you have to do, after you learn the sextant, is to hold it steady and measure the angle of the sun above the horizon as precisely as the rolling of the ship permits (It's best to take about three sightings and average them out). Then you resort to Norie's Nautical Tables and the Nautical Almanac to find the sun's correction and the sun's declination, do some computations and come out with a latitude reading.

With John's help, a couple of students were able to get results within one cable (600 feet) accuracy. Flushed with success, and assured of our interest, John next turned to mid-morning sun sights, with longitude in mind, and morning and evening star sights.

Fortunately, he'd brought along his cadet notebooks from the 1950s, with their longitude formulas, and the results have been so good that we're sure we can find our way to San Salvador without the GPS. In our hubris, some of us wanted to disable the GPS, but John takes a more lenient view. "Now that we've confirmed its accuracy," he says, "why don't we just keep it as a backup system."

DAY 40
Thursday, 27 March. Noon position: 20-02 N, 42-40 W.
Distance from West Palm Beach: 2,142 miles.

Late yesterday I climbed to the highest point on the *Jeanie Johnston*-- up the ratlines on the main mast shrouds, up a vertical rope ladder to a platform between the main course and topsail yards, up another rope ladder narrowing to a point above the topsail yard, up another that took me past the topgallant yard and still another, until I stood on the royal yard, the highest point on the ship, 90-some feet above the deck.

The sea was a huge flat saucer, and I was at the center of it. The ship below me looked smaller than I thought it would, and

197

our forward motion through the water was barely perceptible.

"Now reach up and touch those last few feet of the mast above your head," said Tom Harding. I did, and cheering broke out from the deck far below. People had apparently been watching my progress.

"You're the oldest person ever to climb to the top of the Jeanie's rigging," said Tom. Back down on the deck, there were high fives from everyone I encountered, but the real reward came at dinner.

The Captain had designated a special "over-65" table so we seniors wouldn't have to fight for table room among all the young bodies. Now he came over with a bottle of his best wine, filled glasses all around and raised his own in a toast.

Our plot now is for one of us to reach the top every day, hopefully luring out a new bottle of wine each time.

After dinner, the celebration moved into the great cabin, where the wine continued to flow, and we ended up drinking Bailey's and telling ghost stories far into the night.

DAY 41
Friday, 28 March. Noon position: 20-28 N, 44-52 W.
Distance from West Palm Beach: 2016 miles.

Prominently displayed now on the wall of the great cabin is the plaque I presented on behalf of the US Coast Guard Auxiliary to the officers and crew of the *Jeanie Johnston*.

In a deck talk, I explained what our 36,000 civilian volunteers do in the Auxiliary, and many were surprised by the scope of the work. Our activities-- public education, vessel inspections, safety patrols, and backup for the US Coast Guard in every role but law enforcement-- these are split up in Ireland among several different jurisdictions.

The Irish Navy does law enforcement at sea-- drugs, illegal immigrants, enforcement of fisheries regulations-- areas covered in the US by our Coast Guard.

The Irish Coast Guard operates control centers and hilltop sites from which they communicate with ships at sea and with rescue units involved in search and rescue operations.

Vessel inspections and other regulatory matters come under the Department of Marine.

The group that is wholly devoted to search and rescue is the Royal National Lifeboat Institution (RNLI), a long-standing heritage from the United Kingdom (UK), which in Ireland is called the Royal National Lifeboat of Ireland.

The RNLI are all volunteers, except for a small core of paid personnel, and they are not supported by the Government. All the dramatic rescues you've heard about in the UK and Ireland over the years were carried out by the RNLI.

The remarkable thing about them is that their modern rescue craft, station buildings and equipment are all financed through their own fund-raising efforts. When the RNLI needs a new rescue boat, they must buy it. A number of the *Jeanie Johnston*'s professional crew are RNLI members as well.

When US Coast Guard Auxiliarists come aboard the *Jeanie* this summer in Baltimore, Philadelphia, New York or Boston, I hope they will ask to see the plaque and identify themselves as Coast Guard Auxiliary members. They'll get a hearty welcome from these fellow members of the brotherhood of the sea.

DAY 42

Saturday, 29 March. Noon position:21-13 N, 46-36 W.
Distance to West Palm Beach: 1,910 miles.

An understanding of tall ship principles is essential for anyone contemplating an ocean voyage on a square-rigged ship.

First you must master the Uncertainty Principle, especially in its relation to the Discomfort Factor. The Uncertainty Principle always affects the Discomfort Factor directly, never inversely.

Thus if things could get worse, they will. If things could get better, the Uncertainty Principle ensures that they won't.

This is sometimes called Murphy's Law of the Sea.

Life at sea is governed by an invisible force (the wind), and while the wind operates in accordance with the laws of nature, those laws are often affected capriciously by the Uncertainty Principle.

Thus if the Captain says we shouldn't go any farther south, because we're already far enough south, and a few hours later, you find the ship turning south, that is the Uncertainty Principle at work. It directly affects the Discomfort Factor in this way: If you were sweaty-hot in your bunk last night, you will be sweatier-hot tonight.

Be assured that the Captain and all the crew are acting in good faith, but they, the ship and everyone on it are at the mercy of the Uncertainty Principle.

All the ship's systems, in fact, are affected by this principle. The air conditioning, for example, can not be used to relieve the crew's sweaty-hot state because it consumes fuel, and if the fuel were used up and the Uncertainty Principle caused the wind to die, and the ship came to a stop, then the thousands of visitors waiting ashore to view the ship's interior in air-conditioned comfort would not only be deprived of their viewing but would themselves soon be sweaty-hot from waiting in the sun.

Many other useful examples could be cited but these will have to suffice because it is too hot to write any more. Remember, an understanding of these principles will help to make shipboard life more tolerable.

DAY 43
Sunday, 30 March. Noon position: 21-31 N, 49-01 W.
Distance to West Palm Beach-- 1,773 nautical miles

The weather has changed-- and changed again. The trade wind, pushing us along nicely, reversed itself and blew hard on our bow. For two days, it held there, while we motored with furled sails. Then, about 0600 today, it reversed again and blew with a vengeance. We got square sails up-- courses and top-sails-- and in a few minutes were making almost nine knots. But then big seas arose, and we've had rolling and lurching that matches the worst of the Fenit-Madeira run.

For our new crop of young sail trainees, this is their baptism of fire. They are looking pale and running for the rail. On the mess deck, at breakfast, dishes flew from the table, then some of the food. In no time, the floor was slick with grease and porridge, feet flew out from under legs and bodies crashed.

In the great cabin, cupboard doors flew open and wine glasses, one after the other, popped out and smashed themselves in a ghostly toast; while Sarah the cook's pet goldfish flew through the air, tank and all, to crash and slither on the floor. Jim grabbed the fish while Richard filled a water tumbler to give them temporary quarters. They now live in a plastic kitchen storage box on the book shelf, protected from falling out by a fiddle rail. Whether they feel more at home among *The Famine Ship Diary, The Art of Rigging, Square Rigged Sailing Ships, Famous Sea Stories* and *Anam Cara-- a Book of Celtic Wisdom*, we can only guess.

Being on deck seemed safer for us than being below, but then some of the outdoor mess tables and benches broke their lashings and slid menacingly across the deck. At that point, the Captain ordered everyone below decks.

By lunch time there was no let-up; if anything, the lurches were faster and nastier. A member of the 12 to 4 watch, trying to catch a little sleep, was seen to rise from his bunk in an involuntary levitation. Gavin, carrying a teapot, lost his footing and the teapot flew, splattering three people. Others came to the rescue and ended up in a pileup of bodies at the next roll.

In the galley, a vast lurch brought dozens of plates and bowls rising out of their overhead racks, and all hands reached up to hold them in place.

But all these inconveniences-- heart-stopping as they may be at the moment-- are only the necessary evils of a challenging ocean voyage. We have almost 30 knots of wind on our starboard quarter and are doing some seven-and-a-half knots through short, 12-foot seas. From the top of the aft deckhouse the view is spectacular as the ship rises with the swells, plows into the troughs and sends tons of white water cascading.

DAY 44

Monday, 31 March. Noon position: 21-47 N, 51-33 W.
Distance to West Palm Beach: 1,631 miles.

There are more stars out here than most city-dwellers in New Jersey, New York or Pennsylvania have ever seen. These are the stars that the people of the ancient world knew well, arranged in patterns that had special meanings for them. But we have left the visible skies and the stories they told far behind, smothered in our industrial pollution and rendered archaic by the wonders revealed through the Hubble telescope.

What we see out here is a kind of time warp, a piece of ancient history-- the heroes and gods that occupied ancient minds, the guideposts that led ancient mariners to safe landfalls.

In this sky, the constellations are all laid out, each in its proper place, brilliantly visible. They are alive and vital, and they still have a story to tell.

In the dark of the afterdeck, John Gill takes us on a guided tour, using his flashlight as a cosmic pointer. We start with the Milky Way, the great wheel of our own galaxy, move to the Big Dipper and Polaris, the pole star; Leo, the Lion; The Pleiades; The Twins; Orion; Cassiopeia.

"There's Taurus, the Bull," says John, pointing, and as I look at it I suddenly have a revelation.

Our skies at home are flat, with stars seemingly plastered on them. This sky, with its total clarity, has dimension. I see not only the stars of the Taurus constellation; I see for the first time the bull's blazing eyes and flaring nostrils, the tilt of its head, the way its muzzle juts out at me. I am seeing Taurus as a Greek or Phoenician seaman would have seen it, and I can appreciate the effect it must have had on him.

DAY 45
Tuesday, April 1. Noon position: 22-11 N, 53-20 W.
Distance to West Palm Beach: 1,528 miles.

After my climb to the royal yard, the Captain has banned the voyage crew from going any higher than the "table"-- the platform above the course yard on either the mainmast or foremast.

Tom Harding described the aftermath of my rash excursion: "Yankee Tom's visit to the royal yard and then casually standing upright on same as he patted the mast top, when just one month short of his 82nd birthday, shamed all the young ones, so there ensued a stampede to try to equal his feat."

The Captain's decision probably is a wise precaution considering where we are-- more than 1,000 miles from land in any direction. Any serious injury resulting from a fall would have to be dealt with on the ship since we are well beyond the range of rescue helicopters.

We have been very lucky thus far. For the first 10 days out of Fenit, we thought there must be bones everywhere just waiting to be broken. But most people managed to grab something before they were toppled, and we got off with a few cracked ribs, a couple of sprained ankles and an assortment of minor gashes and bruises. Ship's doctor Tom McCormack was most in demand for dispensing sleeping pills and seasickness tablets.

While we are still a long way from the Sargasso Sea, patches of sargassum weed have been visible in the water for some time. They are yellowish in color and formed into loose clumps. I wonder how the weeds can be floating so far east of the Sargasso Sea when the current here is moving to the west.

Captain McCarthy has the answer: they are formed in the waters off Africa, drift west in the North Equatorial Current and come to rest in the giant eddy formed at the confluence of the Gulf Stream and two other currents. There an entire ecosystem thrives on vast rafts of the weed.

Jim Callery and I saw the green flash the other night-- he for the first time and I for the third. I was startled when it happened-- a sort of bow-tie effect, with the momentary flash fanning out on either side and disappearing like a strobe light. Now we have the entire ship's company watching for the flash.

DAY 46
Wednesday, 2 April. Noon position: 22-43 N, 55-32 W.
Distance to West Palm Beach: 1,402 miles.

Our second week of following Columbus's track from Gomera to San Salvador was completed last Saturday, and I have been trying to make some meaningful comparisons, but it's proving difficult to do so.

The record of our progress is specific and detailed. With the help of global positioning satellites, we know where we are at any given moment and where we were at any time in the past. What we know of Columbus's progress is pitifully little by comparison.

His journal was lost centuries ago, and all we have is an abstract of a copy of it. Las Casas, who made his abstract in 1552, appeared himself to mistrust the copy from which he worked. In reporting distances, he frequently adds the expression, "if the copy be not corrupt." He appears at times to

204

be guessing, with expressions like "they must have made 39 leagues," or "some 20 or 30 leagues."

Add to these uncertainties the charges some critics have aimed at Las Casas, accusing him of falsifying the journal to suit his own views, and the prospects of having the truth are dim. Translating Columbus's leagues into nautical miles and giving him the benefit of every doubt, I put his progress in the second week at 794 nautical miles against our 898. But I suspect the difference is much greater.

Columbus had no charts, and his methods of dead reckoning were imprecise. The ocean is now well charted and Capt. McCarthy, an acknowledged expert in tides and currents, is taking advantage of every ocean feature to advance our progress. My conclusion: let's salute Columbus but abandon the comparisons.

The Captain, in turn, has wisely decided to concentrate on the symbolism of the Columbus voyage rather than its details. He has announced a "Rodrigo de Triana" award for the first person who sights land. Rodrigo was a sailor on the Pinta who held that distinction originally. Whether he received the 10,000 maravedis annually promised by the King and Queen, the journal doesn't say. The Captain, for his part, is keeping the nature of his award a close secret.

DAY 47

Thursday, 3 April. Noon position: 22-53 N, 57-47 W.
Distance to West Palm Beach: 1,277 miles.

We look at the sea day after day and we see very little.

Since the voyage started, three or four ships have been sighted, only one close enough to make out any detail. It's a lonely sea, and we probably all have a secret wish that it might be more heavily populated.

Turning inward, we are quite comfortable with the

population density aboard the *Jeanie Johnston*. We 40 know one another well enough by now, and we fit the ship perfectly, occupying all the bunks and compartments fully and getting by in the mess deck and great cabin with one meal sitting.

"I can't imagine what it would be like if we had twice as many," says one. "We'd be tripping over one another. And where would the others sleep? The thought of having 80 people aboard is a little frightening.

Now take a more radical step and double the ship's population again-- to 80 an then to 160. "That would be totally impossible," says one of our numbers. "There would be no place to sleep, there wouldn't be enough heads, and the galley could never serve that many."

Now take the inconceivable step of adding another 33-- bringing the total to 193-- and you have the number that embarked on the original *Jeanie Johnston* on her maiden voyage to Quebec on April 24, 1848.

How could that many people inhabit the same space we do? For one thing, there were no heads. Shared buckets were carried up and emptied overboard. There was no galley. Passengers carried their own cooking utensils and queued up for a turn at the single stove on deck to cook their ration of flour, oatmeal and rice.

How did they sleep? They were, in fact, crammed in, four to a six-foot-square bunk (a foot and a half per person), with two children counting as one adult. We find it hard to believe, but the ship on one voyage carried 254 passengers.

When visitors come aboard this summer, they will see the 'tween deck space, where we sleep, set up as it would have been in the 19th century, with realistic human figures representing the emigrants of that day.

The entire ship will be a history lesson brought to life in a compelling way that no one who sees it will ever forget.

206

DAY 48

Friday, 4 April. Noon position: 23-29 N, 60-03 W.
Distance from West Palm Beach: 1,149 miles.

There's a spirit abroad on the ship that's hard to describe. It's best seen in quick casual glimpses here and there. Conversations are more spirited, feet move more quickly, sunrises and sunsets draw more keen viewers, the Captain is seen with a broad smile on his face. We are rapidly approaching our destination, and spirits are rising with each mile.

We still hope to visit San Salvador, but giving up the Columbus comparisons has taken a load off everyone's mind. Every true Irishman, after all, knows the New World was discovered by St. Brendan in the sixth century-- in a leather boat at that. And of one thing we can all be certain: this is an Irish ship.

The dialects range from Dublin to Cork to Donegal, but they all lilt, and the stories they tell bring gales of laughter to everyone. On the deck talk schedule, along with navigation and maintenance, is a presentation on the Irish Famine, by Jim Callery, who founded the National Famine Museum, and another entitled "A Bit of Irish Language," by Peter O'Regan, engineering officer and a fluent Irish speaker. On the door to the below-decks space where Peter's diesel engines and generators wait in quiet obedience for his commands is a sign in Gaelic, "SEOMRA na nINNEALL," or "Room of the Engine."

Irishness pervades every aspect of shipboard life, and I find the Irish ethos easy to absorb, so I must occasionally get off by myself just to safeguard my own identity.

Imagine dinner conversations in the US centering typically on US history. Here Irish history is a staple at the dinner table. Night after night, there are lively discussions of the Battle of Kinsale, the Flight of the Wild Geese, the Battle of the Boyne, and always, the Great Potato Famine, the episode of Irish history that is responsible for the ship's existence. When music is played, there are sure to be Irish ballads that speak of separation and yearning, and of blood spilled in lost battles.

In the great Irish diaspora, voyage after voyage took Irishmen to the corners of the earth, where they often played leading roles in the history of foreign nations. Book after book has been written about the Irish in Europe, in Australia, in America.

This voyage is different from all those in the past. It will bring a piece of Ireland to America, but it will not be dissipated; it will remain intact. The *Jeanie Johnston*, a cocoon of Irish history and culture, will travel from port to port and then return to Ireland. My advice to Americans: grab the experience when you can, before it slips away. It will enrich your life.

DAY 49

Saturday, 5 April. Noon position: 23-09 N, 62-27 W.
Distance from West Palm Beach: 1,011 miles.

When nothing special is happening on the ship, there's still plenty going on.

There are watches to be kept (12-4, 4-8, 8-12, 12-4, 4-8, 8-12), meals to be made, cleaning to be done, and maintenance to be kept up.

The basic schedule is posted in the wheel house: "0600-- call cook; 0645-- call galley rats; 0715--call 8-12 watch; 0730--breakfast, 1st sitting for ongoing watch; 0800-- second sitting; 0845-- call 12-4 watch for cleaning stations; crew meeting at the wheel; 0900-1000-- Happy Hour (wiping, vacuuming, hosing, swabbing); 1000-1230-- Lecture/drill/work; 1300-1500--Silence! (The Captain retires to his cabin); Lunch is at 1230 and dinner at 1730; video hours in the great cabin--1600- 2000.

Those who are on watch when sails are changed do the changing, but sometimes when sails must be changed quickly to meet a new weather condition, all hands may be called. During the worst of the gales, only permanent crew members went aloft, and they were augmented during the Fenit-Madeira run by several sailing cadets. Voyage crew members who have felt comfortable doing so have gone aloft at less demanding times. Everyone at one time or another has taken part in cleanup and dressing up the ship.

Maintenance of the ship's spaces and systems takes place all the time, regardless of what else is happening. Engineer Peter O'Regan changes his engines' oil every 250 hours, makes adjustments frequently and keeps detailed records. First officer Rob Matthews leads work crews in sanding, oiling and varnishing. Much of this has been done but much remains. Before we dock at West Palm Beach, our decks must be cleaned and topsides painted.

In the little chunks of time left over, Bosun Tom Harding and Bosun's Mate Dave Nolan fashion new sail gaskets out of braided rope, and the sail trainees cut rope into short lengths to produce "baggywrinkles," which look something like giant soft shoe brushes about two feet long. They're installed at key points in the rigging to prevent chafing of the sails.

But this list merely scratches the surface. The fact is that the work of keeping up a wooden ship is never done.

DAY 50
Sunday, 6 April. Noon position: 23-24 N, 64-43 W.
Distance fom West Palm Beach: 882 miles.

The trade wind is in full force, and we are making the most of it. The ideal place for the wind relative to the course we want to sail is 60 degrees off our stern, and the wind has been there for three days, on our port quarter. We've done eight-and-a-half knots briefly and have clocked six-and-a-half for long periods.

Yesterday saw more activity than usual. Whales were sighted, including one that breached (leaped clear of the water), and we were stalked by a British Navy ship, *Black Rover* out of London. It came up behind us at great speed and quite obviously came over close to take a look, then crossed our bow and resumed its course. The Captain signaled "Hello" with the ship's horn but it took two tries to get a perfunctory answer. We made it out to be a supply ship of some sort.

On the mess deck last night, a half dozen of us got into a discussion of why we were here. Gavin Buckley, a lawyer from Dublin, had been working too hard when he saw a photo of a boat in one of the round-the-world races streaking through the Great Southern Ocean, and it appeared to him incredibly romantic. When the *Jeanie Johnston* announcement came along, Gavin, a non-sailor, was ready.

Tom and Maura Cannon, our only married couple, who live in retirement near the sea and have always loved sea stories, saw the voyage as the culmination of a life-long interest.

Carmel Smith had an adventurous streak buried for years under the responsibilities of marriage and motherhood, and it finally broke loose.

Jim Callery is a successful businessman and property owner with a long career in autos, trucks and farm equipment. He bought an old manor house and found in its attic a trove of 19th century letters from and about victims of the famine who fled Ireland to Quebec, dying by the hundreds on "coffin" ships and in Quebec's infamous Grosse Ile quarantine area. Jim was so moved that he turned part of the estate into the National Famine Museum. Now he is trying to understand what a 19th century ocean voyage would have been like.

For my part, there is, of course, my grandmother, Joanna O'Brien, along with the joy of sailing and the love of my own boat *Second Wind*. There's also a deeply-embedded vision of square-rigged ships, probably planted in my youth by Errol Flynn leaping from the ratlines, sword in hand, and fanned in later years by the novels of Patrick O'Brian.

DAY 51

Monday, 7 April. Noon position: 23-57 N, 66-49 W.
Distance from West Palm Beach: 761 Miles.

We have viewed our ship at last in all her white-clothed majesty, and, individually and collectively, we are awed beyond belief. She may well be the most beautiful thing we have ever seen.

It's a truism among sailors that they have no idea what their vessel looks like under sail to a spectator a half mile away.

The right circumstances-- wind, weather, and sea-- had never come together for proper photographs of the *Jeanie Johnston*. Now they have.

Paul Dolan, Director of the TV and Video Production Unit of FAS, the Irish Training and Employment Agency of Tralee, has been chasing this dream for months.

Yesterday, the fates were in alignment. Weather, wind and sea were perfect, and the Captain decided the time was right to give Paul his big chance.

Launching the rescue boat from its stern davit requires bringing the ship virtually to a halt. The wind was on our starboard quarter, so the yards on both foremast and mainmast were braced back to port. The ship was first maneuvered to bring the wind on its beam. Then all yards on the mainmast were braced back to starboard. The sails on one mast were now canceling out the drive of the sails on the other, and the ship gradually slowed, almost stopping.

The boat was launched, brought alongside and Paul and his gear were taken aboard. The original sail trim and direction were then resumed, and for a half hour Paul circled the ship, shooting photos and video footage from every angle.

Later, he displayed some of the photos for us on his laptop

computer, and we saw for the first time the sheer beauty of the *Jeanie Johnston* under full sail. My favorite shot is one in which a large swell interevenes between camera and ship.

DAY 52
Tuesday, 8 April. Noon Position: 24-16 N, 69-09 W.
Distance to West Palm Beach: 632 miles.

Our watch leader, Mark Tighe, who has been trolling a line off the stern, this morning pulled in a beautiful silvery dorado about three feet long. We estimated its weight at a bit over 30 pounds. Everyone ran to get cameras, and Mark posed proudly with the fish. Then Tom Harding and the Captain, the other fishermen who had been tending the lines, took their turns. That set off some of the young sail trainees, and a half dozen or so were photographed with the big fish they didn't catch.

Sarah examined it. By now, its bright silver was fading to a splotchy patchwork of color. "It will feed us all." she said. The next step, if we were to have it fresh, was to reduce the fish to cooking portions.

Tom Harding, always handy with a knife, began the process, and it was taken up by young Darren from Northern Ireland, who had once worked in a fish factory in the Killebegs fishing port in Donegal.

I admired the fish when it was held aloft, and I will undoubtedly eat it with relish, but I had no desire to see it dismembered. As most of the others gathered around to watch, I puzzled about this. The answer, I think, is that no one else on the ship, from the teen-agers up to 74-year-old Tom of the voyage crew, has ever lived through a war.

Something tells me I do not need to see blood on the deck. This is a deep-seated, almost unconscious reaction that my friends at the Rutgers Oral History Archives of World War II will understand if others cannot. They and I have long since

212

unburdened ourselves of our wartime memories in extensive interviews, and those memories are now displayed on the Internet, where scholars are mining them for new insights.

By and large, we live at peace with ourselves, but occasionally something-- like the fish-- may cause the door to that underground vault to crack open slightly.

DAY 53

*Wednesday, 9 April. Noon position: 24-02 N, 72-02 W.
Distance to West Palm Beach: 471 miles.*

Sarah Caffery, our cook, sometimes wonders how she got herself into this job on a square-rigged ship, which at best offers a somewhat primitive cooking environment. In a deck talk today, she gave us some clues.

Back home in Ireland, Sarah lives a normal life as a primary school teacher. Her pupils may sometimes give her problems, that's true, but they could never match the challenges she faces on the *Jeanie Johnston*.

The route that led her to the ship started with work in three restaurants and led to service as a cook in a transatlantic race. Then she heard of the JJ and last year got herself qualified as a full-fledged ship's cook.

The voyage, she admits, is a learning experience. She was told in her training that 100 grams of meat and potatoes per person per day was a good rule of thumb. We've been eating double that amount. Sarah estimates we're putting away between 2,500 and 3,000 calories daily. The food is varied, and it's always good.

Since we left Fenit on February 16, we've consumed half a ton of potatoes and 500 liters of milk. Breakfast, often considered the smallest meal of the day, consistently features porridge, bacon, eggs, sausage, grapefruit, orange juice, toast and fresh-baked scones.

Stocking the ship was Sarah's first problem. She utilized space wherever she could find it-- in the tank room, great cabin lockers, forepeak, under the floor everywhere.

A visitor to the ship in Ireland asked her how she liked the galley. "It's too small," she said. The visitor turned out to be the naval architect who had designed the ship. "Next time, I'll make a bigger galley," he told her.

A normal day in the galley is challenge enough. The gales were something else. "Food came flying out of the fridge three times in one day," she said, "and the galley helpers were clinging to the rim of the sink."

Sarah herself went flying at least once, with her cook's knife in her hand. The galley's radio was smashed, two percolators were rendered useless and uncounted numbers of bowls and plates were smashed to bits.

The ship's time in the US will be a breeze, with easy three-day voyages in coastal waters, and probably no great sailing challenges. Then, in the fall, there will be the long voyage home. Sarah is on sabbatical, and her job is waiting for her. She should have some interesting tales to tell her pupils.

DAY 54
Thursday, 10 April. Noon position: 23-55 N, 74-24 W.
Distance to West Palm Beach: 340 miles.

Jim Callery came aboard the ship with more expensive gadgets than I'd ever seen on one person. Jim had been loaded down by his family with cameras, recorders, video cams and most notably, an Iridium satellite phone-- the kind journalists use increasingly to send reports from the remote corners of the world.

Jim had only a shaky foothold on the world of computers and electronics, but he is blessed with an insatiable curiosity and a fierce determination. A non-sailor, he has doggedly read a

214

square-rigged sailor's manual three times in an effort to cram knowledge into his head.

He waded into the armful of manuals that came with his electronic gadgets and before long, with a little trial-and-error, he was using them all, including the satellite phone. The phone, on loan from Barry Electronics, a firm in Killybegs, County Donegal, that supplies marine electronics to the fishing industries, is truly a wonder.

You can go on deck, pull out the little antenna, dial your number and talk with someone on land 2,000 miles away. I called my wife Marie and heard her voice as clearly as I would on a local telephone line. Other members of the crew used the phone as well. There were times, of course, when through no fault of the phone, the satellite coverage blanked out and the conversation would crackle and break up.

Jim had a phone interview coming up with a radio reporter in Shannonside, Ireland, and it would be an opportunity to credit Barry Electronics for their generous gesture. The interview went off smoothly, but just at the end, when Jim was about to mention Barry's name, the satellite signals seemed to go awry and the coverage broke up.

But there's more than one way to skin a cat. In my daily report for the day, I concluded by saying "From those of us who have enjoyed the phone, thank you, Barry Electronics."

DAY 55

Friday, 11 April. Noon position: 25-17 N, 76-05 W. Distance to West Palm Beach: 211 miles

Yesterday about 1000 we raised the coast of San Salvador, where Columbus made his New World landfall, and for several hours had it on our starboard side.

It took Columbus 36 days from Gomera to San Salvador. It took us 26 days, and the distance covered was 3,342 nautical

215

miles. Columbus took possession of the island for the King and Queen, studied the natives briefly (They were "well built, with very handsome bodies and good faces," he wrote), but then he was eager to move on the the island of Cipangu (Japan), which he assumed was nearby.

Captain McCarthy had thought earlier of anchoring and going ashore, but that was not now practical. The harbors and landing places are on the west side of the island. As we approached, the wind was strong from the northwest, and he had no wish to put his ship in danger by anchoring off a lee shore. So we continued to the northwest under power and during the night skirted Cat Island off our port side.

Today we continue on the same course, under power with staysails up for stability. A 24-knot wind is hard on our port bow, so there is no way to make headway by sail alone. The coast of Eleuthera is now remotely visible off our port side as we head for the north East Providence Channel and Nassau.

I remember Eleuthera from having spent a couple of weeks there in January, 1970, when the island was experiencing a "norther," the remnants of a big Atlantic storm far to the north. As the northernmost islands in the Western Atlantic, the Bahamas (named by Columbus, *baja mar*, or shallow sea) can sometimes catch ocean swells generated hundreds of miles away.

Signs of civilization are now about us. A long jet trail showed us the route to Nassau's airport, and a monstrous cruise ship went by. Our 19th century idyll is being diluted, and we will soon be reabsorbed by the 21st century.

DAY 56
Saturday, 12 April. Ashore in Nassau. Noon position: 26-14 N, 78-34 W. Distance to West Palm Beach: 78 miles

We picked up the pilot off Nassau at 0745 and by 0830

216

were tied up in cruise ship territory, a tiny wooden boat surrounded by gigantic floating hotels.

The ship directly opposite us, if you looked at it from the side, could have been a block-long condominium building in Miami. All its outside staterooms (if, indeed, they are still called that) have balconies, and we can only imagine what the interior spaces look like.

It doesn't take long to get the drift of things in Nassau: thousands of one-day visitors shouldering their way in and out of t-shirt shops. . .plenty of cold beer. . .amphibian planes and parasailing. . .the Pirates' Den Nightclub directly across the street from the Anglican Cathedral. . .the world's largest pink hotel (Michael Jackson owns the apartment in that famous arch between the two buildings). . .Mick Jagger's house (Where doesn't he have one?). . .enough gleaming white 150-foot motor yachts to carry the whole population out to sea. . .and a total disregard for speed limits and traffic regulations, especially on Saturday night.

After our spartan days at sea, Nassau seemed totally dissolute, and that scofflaw driving attitude almost cost us dearly. As 10 of us made our way back after dinner ashore, one stepped out to cross the street and came within a hair's breadth of being struck by a speeding car. In the flash of a moment, he had to throw his body to the pavement, then roll out of the way. The driver never stopped.

It made us realize how lucky we've been. Imagine crossing the Atlantic on a small wooden ship, fighting through gales, being seasick, struggling to keep from breaking bones as everything crashed about you, and then being hit by a car when you're virtually within shouting distance of home. It almost happened.

Were we glad to be back in civilization? At that moment, we couldn't be sure.

217

DAY 57
Sunday, 13 April. Ashore in Nassau

Jim Callery and I took a room in the Hilton Hotel and slept a long, luxurious sleep. When we woke, it was Palm Sunday. We had a leisurely breakfast, and I bought a copy of the Sunday *New York Times.* Amazing! The *New York Times* on the same day of its publication!

Jim had been up early and discovered a little Anglican church off on a side street and up a hill. He'd chatted with the bishop and found himself part of a parade that included well-dressed people carrying palms, a choir and a marching band. We decided to go back and attend the service.

"We have two visitors," the priest announced, "one from Ireland and one from the United States." The choir was sublime, and though we were in a foreign country, the words were in English.

I thought of our long, safe voyage, with no one seriously hurt on the ship, and no one killed by the speeding car, and I said a prayer of thanksgiving. While I don't believe God favors one person or group over others, I wonder if the *Jeanie Johnston* may somehow be blessed.

Hidden away in a niche in her aft companionway between the bridge and the mess deck is an old, worn little statue of The Child of Prague. It was placed there by a carpenter who worked on the ship, and it had seen duty on one or more old ships during its lifetime. The original Child was said to have saved the city of Prague from war and pestilence. How the idea got to Ireland is a mystery, but I've learned that in Dingle, where Peter O'Regan grew up, such statues are frequently installed on newly built boats to give them a special protection.

When we docked here yesterday, an Irish woman came over to the ship and expressed surprise at seeing us. She said she had bet money that the Jeanie would never make it across the

Atlantic. We looked at her in astonishment. Could whatever Divine Providence there is be bending over backward to offset such lack of faith? We may have reason to believe so.

DAY 58
Enroute from Nassau to West Palm Beach

We are on the home stretch now, and already reminiscences are rife. The idea is sinking in that the voyage is almost over, and that each of us will shortly be pursuing his or her own way.

Captain McCarthy recalls his constant questing for the best of the trade winds, and the frustration of going where he thought they should be and not always finding them. "They're not as reliable as they were in the days of sail," he says sadly.

Jim and I recall-- laughingly now-- the water dripping down on our bunks, and the daily mental chore of trying to guess where items of gear had been stowed. Jim will not forget, either, the stab of pain a day after he cracked his ribs, when someone jostled him at the mess table.

Almost everyone remembers, not too fondly, the green feeling of seasickness.

Offsetting those negatives was the rare experience Jim and I both had-- seeing the "green flash" in all its evanescent glory.

A lucky handful who were looking in the right direction at the right time will never forget seeing the whale breach-- its whole gigantic body seemingly floating in the air.

Someone recounts the hilarious predicament of seasick young Darren, who was retching in his bunk, while water from a deck leak dripped on his head, when Carmel, thrown off balance by a sudden roll, fell into his bunk, spilling her plateful of hot curry and rice over him. "This is the worst day of my entire life," lamented Darren. But he recovered.

Most recall the awe they felt being on deck during the gales, when tons of green water came over the bows and occasionally over the top of the forward deck house.

Virtually all of us remember the thrill we felt the first time all sails were set and filled by a 16- to 20-knot wind.

Everyone has etched in memory his or her own personal near-disaster-- careening across the deck in the wake of a bad roll, reaching to grab a handrail but failing to catch it in time. My worst was smashing my lower ribs against the mizzen mast while trying to walk across the great cabin.

Tom Harding's chief recollection is of fish caught and uncaught: "We were not nearly as successful as our investment in flashy lures and gear might suggest." Of tender-hearted girls who want to throw back flying fish, he says, "It's hard to explain to a lubber that they actively seek our frying pan."

A memory worth keeping is that the long days Tom, Dave Nolan, Mark Tighe and Boyce Nolan put into stitching and rigging the stuns'ls paid off: "Captain Tom reckons they add an extra knot when the breeze is fresh."

Paul Dolan remembers being so discouraged by the early roughness of the voyage that when we reached Madeira he seriously considered canceling his passage for the second half of it.

Sarah Caffery is still astounded that none of her galley crew was injured or scalded carrying hot food down the companionway before ropes and handholds were installed. She remembers one close call after another.

For Dr. Tom McCormack, there are memories of turning dentist for Peter O'Regan and pulling a sore tooth, removing a large splinter from Frida Bjorsell's foot and dispensing more seasick tablets than he ever thought he'd need. But no broken bones, for which he is thankful.

One thing none of us will ever forget is the *Jeanie Johnston* herself. Every wooden inch of her is so etched into our memories that she'll inhabit our dreams, and years from now the young sail trainees will regale their grandchildren with tales of how they crossed the Atlantic on a little wooden ship.

DAY 59
Tuesday, 15 April. Noon position: West Palm Beach.
Distance to West Palm Beach: 0 miles.

The transatlantic adventure is over. This morning, after a voyage of 5,260 miles from Fenit, Ireland, interrupted by stops at Madeira and Tenerife, we picked up the pilot outside the Lake Worth Inlet and headed into West Palm Beach.

The Captain had suggested that I, as the only American aboard, take the wheel as the ship entered the Inlet and made her final approach. I donned my US Coast Guard Auxiliary uniform for the occasion.

The pilot was, of course, directing our course minute by minute, so I was a mere figurehead at the wheel, but it was a proud moment nonetheless. The Coast Guard escorted us in, and dozens of small boats formed a welcoming flotilla. Many of them were probably local Coast Guard Auxiliary, but all we knew of them was that they were wishing us well.

Reporters and photographers on the press boat shouted and waved as they circled the ship, and as we moved in to our dock in the customs area, cruise ships docked nearby gave us a deep-throated blast of welcome.

The crew will be officially discharged on Thursday, but already there have been emotional farewells, exchanges of addresses and talk of a reunion in Tralee at Christmas time. What we have been through together has forged links that most of us are not likely to ever forget.

For me, this marks the culmination of a strange symmetry comprising four years-- 1847, 1863, 1943 and 2003. In 1847, three things happened: (1) the Irish potato famine reached its peak, (2) the original *Jeanie Johnston* was launched, and (3) my grandmother, Joanna O'Brien, was born. In 1863, Joanna

O'Brien emigrated to America. Eighty years later, on April 17, 1943, I embarked on my first Atlantic crossing on the wartime troopship *Andes*. Exactly 60 years after that, on April 17, 2003, I will have completed another Atlantic crossing on the *Jeanie Johnston* (The ship arrived on 15 April but the 17th, when the crew is discharged, is the official end of the voyage.)

Whatever else the voyage may have accomplished, it has surely rendered irrelevant the opinions of those who have been critical of the *Jeanie Johnston* project. The ship and her professional crew have performed beyond all expectations.

Those of us who have seen the Jeanie battle her way through steep seas and fierce gales, her timbers creaking and groaning, never doubted her soundness; nor was there ever any reason to doubt. She has proved herself a triumph of the shipbuilder's art.

It was an honor to have as a shipmate that gentle, self-effacing man, Peter O'Regan. Peter is the ship's engineering officer, but he is much more. He and his brother Ciaran built the ship, employing the oldtime woodworking skills of their family's Dingle shipyard and getting help where they could find it. Theirs is a genius that is rare in today's world.

Another man I am proud to know is John Griffin, who met us here to savor quietly the moment of a lifetime-- seeing the living embodiment of his decade-old vision sail triumphantly into history. John's visionary spirit, and his determination to bring his visions to life, mark him as an extraordinary human being.

Now that the maiden voyage is over, what happens next?

The ship's immediate future is a series of port visits up the US and Canadian coasts (These are listed on the web sites focus-kerry.com/jeanie/ and jeaniejohnston.ie), and in October she will return to Ireland.

After that, her future is uncertain. She could become a sail training ship; she could have a permanent berth as a floating museum; or she could become a Ship of Peace, with mixed

222

crews combining both sides of the world's cultural divides: Catholic/Protestant, Israeli/Palestinian, Hindu/Muslim, black/white, Shiite/Sunni, etc.

To those of us who have voyaged with her, she is a creature of the sea, born to sail and not to sit at the dock. We can see her for a time commemorating the history of the famine and the Irish diaspora, but beyond that we hope she will become that Ship of Peace, making her way to the corners of the earth where divisiveness stifles progress.

If people who are culturally worlds apart can pull ropes together, furl sails together and eat ship's fare together, they will have taken the first step toward a world in which brotherhood prevails. This is a noble vision, and the *Jeanie Johnston* is a noble ship. Long may she sail!

EPILOGUE

Bark that bare me through foam and squall,
You in the storm are my castle wall:
Though the sea should redden from bottom to top,
From tiller to mast she takes no drop;
>   *On the tide-top, the tide-top,*
>   *Wherry aroon, my land and store!*
>   *On the tide-top, the tide-top,*
>   *She is the boat can sail go leor**

Irish, 18th Century
Andrew Magrath, *Boatman's Hymn*
Translated by Samuel Ferguson

*This word has come over into English as *galore*.

Some voyages are routine. This one was not. It had to prove something, and it did. In doing so, it vindicated the faith of hundreds, perhaps thousands, of people who gave of themselves to make it happen.

A venture as complex and highly aspiring as the *Jeanie Johnston* Project requires the talents of dreamers, doers, poets, mechanics, organizers, artists, macro-thinkers and micro-thinkers, those who nourish the old and traditional as well as those who seek answers from the latest technology. In the nature of human endeavor, they will advance their respective viewpoints, sometimes cooperating, frequently clashing. Out of

224

the creative stew thus generated, something can be born that occasionally borders on the miraculous.

When John Griffin first floated the idea of building a replica famine ship that could sail the seven seas, there were many scoffers, but also many who found themselves caught up in the dream. The dreamers may not have fully understood the complexity of the Project, but neither did the scoffers appreciate the staying power of the dreamers nor the strength and validity of their vision. Some supporters fell by the wayside when the going got too difficult, while others learned a few practicalities. And some of those who initially derided the dream ultimately became partisans for the ship.

The process was often a messy one, and those who thought it should have been neater were probably deluding themselves. Human nature seldom works in ideal ways.

In the end, what matters is the final product. As she is, the *Jeanie Johnston* is a glory of history, craftsmanship, culture and the celebration of the human spirit. Considering her prolonged and difficult birth process, she is also a triumph-- and something of a miracle.

ISBN 1412005760